Baseball in Hawai'i

Baseball in Hawai'i

JIM VITTI

The History PRESS

Published by The History Press
Charleston, SC 29403
www.historypress.net

Front cover, bottom: The U.S. Army Sixty-fourth Coast Artillery Battery team, Fort Shafter, Oahu, 1939.

Back cover, middle: In 1947, the New York Giants visited Hawai'i to play some exhibition ball. Pitcher Bill Ayers tried on a coconut papale (hat), lei and hula skirt to see if it might improve his delivery. (Alas, it did not; Bill went 0-3 and was shipped down to finish the season at Jersey City.)

Back cover, bottom: The U.S. Navy (featuring Pee Wee Reese) squared off against the U.S. Army (starring Joe DiMaggio) at Honolulu Stadium in 1944.

First published 2014

Manufactured in the United States

ISBN 978.1.62619.313.0

Library of Congress CIP data applied for.

Contents

Acknowledgements

Thanks to so many individuals who blessed me with the Aloha Spirit on O'ahu: Matthew Yim, DeSoto Brown and the entire staff at the Bishop Museum; Barbara Dunn and Ipo Santos-Bear of the Hawai'ian Historical Society; Gina Vergara-Bautista and everyone else at the Hawai'i State Archives; the staff at the Hawai'i State Library; Judith Bowman of the U.S. Army Museum of Hawai'i; Brian Niiya of the Japanese Cultural Center; Greg Sitar of First Hawai'ian Bank; Gil Tam of the Hawai'i Sports Hall of Fame; Derek Inouchi and Jim Cartwright of the University of Hawai'i; Nelson Okino; and the staff at the Hawai'i War Records Depository. A tip of the *papale* goes also to Arthur Suehiro for his spectacular book *Honolulu Stadium*; Libby Burke of the Lyman House Museum; Wayne Subica of the Hawai'i Plantation & Industrial Museum; and, from another faraway set of isles, the UK's finest—Gary Bedingfield of baseballinwartime.com. *Mahalo* to the all-star team at The History Press, anchored by Jerry Roberts and Will Collicott. Thanks also to the following ballplayers and their families: Bob Borkowski, Lonny Frey, Glenn Goya, Olinda and Pam Hacker, Roy "Wonderboy" Hobbs, Hub Kittle and Wayne Terwilliger.

All photos are courtesy of the Bishop Museum, Hawai'i Plantation & Industrial Museum, Hawai'i State Archives, Hawai'i War Records Depository, Japanese Cultural Center, U.S. Army Museum of Hawai'i, University of Hawai'i and the Bill Loughman Collection unless otherwise credited. Memorabilia appears courtesy of the Jim Allyn Collection—thanks to you and Rophe for always being there.

Introduction

Baseball in Hawai'i, eh? Must be a typo. There's no baseball in Hawai'i! There's baseball in Brooklyn and Boston, Baltimore and the Bronx—but not Honolulu. In Honolulu, there are only beaches and palm trees and a perfect hammock, lazily swaying in the trade breeze, with vacationers lulling away in the shade.

Unless Babe Ruth stood on Waikiki Beach, with Diamond Head as his backdrop, smacking horsehides into the Pacific as awe-struck natives watched 'em sail way up and into the sky before splashdown.

Or Joe DiMaggio, wearing an oddly less familiar uniform (completely devoid of pinstripes), was blasting a few out of a place known as the Termite Palace just a few blocks away.

Unless colorful, cartoon-esque characters like Yogi Berra and Casey Stengel performed their feats on the field (and their language-mangling exploits off the field) for reporters in brightly colored luau shirts.

Or Tony Gwynn, playing a major-league game for the San Diego Padres, belted base hits in Aloha Stadium (yep, the same place where NFL stars play the Pro Bowl). And Barry Bonds, on the way up, smacked home runs in the Pittsburgh organization. And Ichiro, playing for a team in Hilo, socked the cover off the ball.

Not to mention plenty of other all-stars and Hall of Famers (like Lou Gehrig and Mickey Mantle), superstars from Asia (lesser known on the mainland but plenty big back home), some of the best collegiate baseball teams of all time and thousands of locals, guys who used machetes to harvest pineapples and fellas who drove trucks from sugar fields, on Plantation League teams whose contests were legend and whose rivalries were intense. They pitched and caught and swung away, got in the volcanic dirt and the grass and shaded their eyes against the tropical afternoon sunshine to make a circus catch within earshot of waves crashing nearby.

Yeah, baseball in Hawai‘i.

The funny thing is, baseball came to Hawai‘i before it arrived in a lot of traditional, old-school American cities. It seems Alexander Cartwright, who pretty much devised the game as we know it, moved to the Isles just a few short years after setting things up back in New York. So, if you look real hard, you can find a diamond in a park hidden in a nondescript neighborhood in Honolulu, a park whose dimensions were literally marched off by the "Father of Baseball" himself. (And that was long before there was a major-league game back across the Pacific Pond.) If you head a few blocks farther along, you'll even find his grave site—constantly graced with caps and balls and notes from loving fans who make the trek from their beachfront resorts to pay their grateful respects.

Since Hawai‘i was always such a transcontinental melting pot, it was natural for baseball to be integrated early on here—decades before Jackie Robinson broke the color line in North America. Sandlot teams, often semipro, were as colorblind as can be in the Plantation Leagues and the Hawai‘i Baseball League. And some of these local teams from the AJA (Americans of Japanese Ancestry) and other civic groups proved good enough to barnstorm from Hawai‘i, globetrotting their talents on multiple continents.

Islanders got their first glimpses of big-league stars long before Pearl Harbor, when off-season touring squads stopped here before continuing on to Japan. Japanese teams came over from the other way, and the games were on.

During the war, plenty of stars were stationed locally, and they put on exhibitions that drew major-league-size crowds. After the war, the major-league convoys resumed.

In 1961, Honolulu landed its first official professional team: the Hawai‘i Islanders. Since it was the highest level of minor-league ball—Triple A—plenty of major-leaguers shuttled up and down throughout each season. Future stars made their marks here en route to lengthy careers, while others gave it one last shot in Hawai‘i before hanging it up. The Islanders remained a firm fixture for twenty-seven seasons, until the franchise moved back to the mainland after the 1987 season.

During that time (and since), the University of Hawai'i became a collegiate powerhouse, other college teams emerged, other leagues came about (like the Hawai'i Winter Baseball League), the big leagues made a brief weekend stopover and, of course, kids and grown-up kids just played for the fun of it and the love of the game in cities and towns and across the countryside on O'ahu, the Big Island, Maui, Kaua'i, Moloka'i and even little Lāna'i.

So, welcome to *Baseball in Hawai'i*. Enjoy the vacation into the stories and photos that will bring the adventure alive.

Note: We have made an editorial decision to respect 'Olelo Hawai'i, the native Hawai'ian language, in how we present Hawai'ian words. For example, you've likely noticed that "Hawaii" instead appears as "Hawai'i." Technically a consonant, the mark that looks like a reversed apostrophe is called the 'okina. The 'okina acts as a glottal stop, meaning that you'd pronounce the word "a-VAi-ee," with a distinctive pause at the beginning. (Note also that there's no true hard "H" in the Hawai'ian language, so the English "hah" sound is absent from the beginning of the word.

CHAPTER 1
BEGINNINGS

Baseball in Hawai'i actually happened before baseball in most of America. The guy who invented our game migrated to the Isles not long after laying things out in New York—so it ironically bypassed most of the country to arrive in Hawai'i first. In those pre-technology years, it took a long time to work its way down from the Northeast into the Midwest and the South and out to the West Coast. Plenty of time passed while things were already evolving in paradise.

So, if you know where to look, Hawai'i is a treasure-trove of early baseball history, and much of it predates the National League's birth in 1876.

The National Baseball Hall of Fame calls Alexander Joy Cartwright the "Father of Modern Baseball." He pretty much invented the game as we know it (nine players, nine innings, size of the diamond) and showed everyone how it was done (with his 1845 New York Knickerbockers). "Alick" moved to Hawai'i just four years later, planting baseball seeds on the Islands, too. He'd left New York to join the gold rush in California but kept heading west until he landed in O'ahu.

Cartwright took trains and covered wagons and rode on horseback and walked (a lot) to cross the continent. It took him five long, dusty months, but he finally made it to the West Coast. After meeting up with his brother in San Francisco, he bought a ticket to paradise; the Peruvian SS *Pacifico* was bound for the Sandwich Islands (as they were then known, so-named by Captain Cook in honor of the Earl of Sandwich). Today, most people live on the half dozen principal islands—O'ahu, Maui, the Big Island of Hawai'i, Kaua'i, Moloka'i

Alexander Cartwright in Hawai'i.

and Lāna'i—but in reality, the chain consists of 137 islands, islets and atolls.

Like so many others, Cartwright fell in love with the place and then sent for his family (a wife, two daughters and a son) and in they settled. The couple had two more sons while living in Hawai'i. And starting with his own sons, Cartwright made sure he taught baseball to anyone who'd lend a moment.

While in Hawai'i, Cartwright did a lot more than spread the word about his newfangled game. He wore more hats than any person could reasonably expect, he was a friend of the movers and shakers there, and he ultimately spent most of his life on O'ahu (more than forty years, in fact)—never moving back to the mainland.

Alick marked off several baseball diamonds around Hawai'i, and most experts think the first was Cartwright Park—still in use today at the corner of Kinau and Keeaumoku Streets, next to the freeway (can't technically call it an "interstate" here!). This venue is about one mile due north of Waikiki. (It was called Makiki Reserve when his boots marked the base paths.)

The locals took up the sport in a hurry; it bore a few vague similarities to a Polynesian game called *aipuni* (which fielded two batters at the same time). The kids used branches from candlenut (kukui) trees to swat at dried-out coconut shells or balls cobbled together from anything they could find.

The mapmakers tell us there's another Cartwright Field just a few miles away, although locals simply know it as the diamond at William McKinley High School. (Historians note the irony that a school in Hawai'i would be named after the man who oversaw its "annexation" in 1898.)

When he wasn't marking off baseball diamonds, Cartwright kept busy improving Hawai'i in a number of other ways, his large cleat prints surviving even to this day. Pivotal in creating the national library, he was also a teacher and a charter director of First Hawai'ian Bank. He aided the king and queen in their (literal) door-to-door campaign to start a hospital and helped develop the Hawai'ian national postal service. Somehow, he also managed to help start the Honolulu Fire Department—where he volunteered as well, becoming certified as an active member of Mechanic Engine Company No. 2 in 1859. Despite all these achievements, he was later lost in bureaucratic red tape at city hall; a marker honoring his achievements that once occupied an interior wall was removed years ago and disappeared into oblivion.

Cartwright Park (top/middle) and Cartwright Field (bottom).

Locals played plenty of pickup games in Hawai'i after Cartwright came, but the first "official" matchup was between a team called the "Foreigners" and its opponents, the "Natives," in 1866. The game took place on the grounds of what's now the Central Union Church, in northern Honolulu (it was called the Seamen's Bethel in those days).

It wasn't just a man's game on the Isles; Honolulu's *Pacific Commercial Advertiser* reported on an 1867 game in which the Pacifics beat the Pioneers 11–9...with more than one hundred ladies in attendance. And the sport quickly spread to the other islands. William Castle, of Castle & Cooke, wrote about watching a game in Waiohinu town (on the Big Island) in the late 1860s.

Cartwright touched a lot more than baseball in Hawai'i. *From top to bottom*: the state library, the main post office and the Queen's Medical Center—all parts of his long-lasting legacy.

King Kalākaua took in his first game in 1875, observing a marathon affair as the Athletes beat the Pensacolas 38–33. (We trust both teams began scouting for bullpen help afterward.) The first recorded inter-island game took place in 1883, when the Honolulu Athletic Club hosted Maui's Sprecklesville team and won 33–16.

The first league, in 1884, consisted of four teams: the Honolulus, the Married Men, the Oceanics and the Pacifics. This semi-organized group played its games at Cartwright's diamond at Makiki Reserve.

Another Hall of Fame baseball pioneer, Al Spalding, assembled a team of all-stars (along with his Chicago White Stockings) for a world baseball tour in the offseason of 1888–89. One of his stops was Cartwright's Sandwich Islands, where he dropped in on the pioneer to talk about the intricacies of the game—and the dark clouds that were looming over local politics.

On the mainland, many Americans don't realize that Hawai'i was an independent nation until President McKinley's marines marched in. Kamehameha was a true king, and the old palace in Honolulu is the only royal palace on U.S. soil. So, Cartwright was actually introducing baseball to another country when he lived there.

Hawaiian princess Victoria Kaiulani, a friend of Cartwright's.

A group of American and European businessmen staged a coup and took over the island in 1893 (calling it a "republic") as Washington turned a blind eye, hands well sweetened by sugar cane and pineapple profits. Princess Victoria Kaiulani was the heiress to the ill-fated Hawai'ian throne at the time. (She was quite well versed in another Hawai'ian sport; as a teenager in England, she showed the locals how to surf—perhaps the very first surfer girl ever). She traveled to the White House to plead with President Grover Cleveland, who was sympathetically swept away by her charm, but she was rebuffed by the Senate. When the United States officially "annexed"

Cartwright's burial site in Honolulu.

her kingdom five years later, she and her family wore funeral attire to the celebration ceremony. Within weeks, she died of a broken heart, at the age of twenty-four.

Cartwright missed all that drama. He died in Hawai'i on July 12, 1892, at age seventy-two. He's buried at the O'ahu Cemetery in Honolulu's Nuuanu Valley, where a large monument marks the site of his family plot. On a regular basis, fans leave caps and balls and other baseball mementos at one of fandom's overlooked shrines. In fact, that's been going on for decades—while on the Isles during his barnstorming tours in the 1930s, Babe Ruth once placed a wreath at Cartwright's grave.

After Alick: Islandball Thrives

After the clubs started their leagues in Honolulu, teams from different plantations started playing against one another, too. The *Hawai'ian Gazette* wrote up the Kaua'i championship from 1897, in which Kealia was pitted against Kilauea. They got official in 1916, when the O'ahu Plantation Athletic Association began sanctioning the contests.

Passions ran high. In 1912, some Hilo residents complained that some of the locals had converted a cemetery into a baseball field. In Honolulu, there were generally more options—like Aala Park, between downtown and the docks. Aala Park is used more for skateboarding now, after falling into disrepair and recently being reclaimed by concerned residents.

Numerous amateur teams sprang up all over the Islands, like the first Japanese team in 1899. The Excelsiors were an outgrowth of Makiki Christian Church, which is why their minister, Takie Okumura, is considered the father of American-Japanese baseball on the Islands.

Other ethnic groups suited up, too, including the (Portuguese) Braves, (*Haole*) Wanderers and the (Japanese) Asahi. (*Haole* literally means "foreigner," and today it can be used both as a general description and a racial epithet, depending on the context.) Their competitors, the Commercial League, included teams from Honolulu Iron Works, O'ahu Sugar and Mutual Telephone, among others.

Waseda University catcher Nagano, visiting Hawai'i from Japan, models the latest in shinguards alongside infielder Kuji in 1911.

The Americans of Japanese Ancestry (AJA) has been a dominant force in "Islandball" for more than a century. Its players originally suited up in 1905, and the AJA Baseball League first fielded competitions in 1908. In 1915, the Asahi ("Rising Sun") Red Sox beat everybody and then barnstormed to Japan for fresh competition. (The Asahi ballplayers saw some familiar faces when they toured in Japan, since the Waseda University team had first made a trip from Tokyo to Hawai'i in 1905.)

In 1924, Asahi became a charter member of the Hawai'i Baseball League. Throughout the century, the Red Sox won nearly two dozen titles and traveled to Asia ten more times. An Asahi-laden all-star team even beat 1974 World Champ Cuba in Japan in front of twenty-five thousand!

Asahi founder Steere Gikaku Noda was also the squad's big star—both on the mound and behind the plate. He was also instrumental in orchestrating the team's international tours. After his playing days, Noda served in Hawai'i's Territorial House and Senate, just prior to statehood. He's enshrined in the Hawai'i Sports Hall of Fame.

Other stars arose. Johnny Nakagawa, a California kid, was often called the Nisei Babe Ruth. ("Nisei" is used to describe someone born in America but of Japanese ancestry.) He hit a four-hundred-foot homer out of Honolulu Stadium in 1927 during a game against the U.S. Navy team. Ruth's batboy's eyes were wide: "Pound for pound, the Nisei players were as good as the major-leaguers," he said years later.

And although many of the teams were ethnically based, they played against one another and fielded plenty of mixed-heritage teams. Hawai'i beat the Major Leagues to integration by decades. One of those integrated teams, calling itself the Hawai'ian Travelers, toured the mainland from 1912 to 1916—playing dozens of games in dozens of cities and towns.

Some of the stiffest competition came within the now firmly established Plantation Leagues, which generated fierce and often bloody rivalries.

An integrated Honolulu team, 1910.

The bigger companies had multiple teams, pitting departments against one another, like truck drivers against sugarcane cutters. Some managers even recruited the top local high school kids, offering jobs in their department, in order to win more ballgames. Plantation League games were held on all the islands, wherever a Cartwright-specified diamond could be leveled and cut out from the crops.

Moiliili Field.

In town, Moiliili Field was also a popular site for ballgames. It's on the northeast corner of King and Isenberg Streets, across the same intersection that later became home to Honolulu Stadium (on the southwest corner). And baseball still breaks out there from time to time, with multiple Cartwright-drawn diamonds in place.

The University of Hawai'i got started in 1907, and within a decade, intramural baseball teams were suiting up. Integrated Warrior squads would take on as many of the barnstormers as they could, and the school finally entered the ranks of NCAA Division I competition in 1971 (when Les Murakami arrived). The first UH alum to sign a pro contract was Neal Blaisdell (class of '23), followed by Ted Nobriga ('32). Both played briefly in the minors on the mainland.

In 1923, the University of California's team came over to play a series of games in both Hilo and Honolulu. These matches were followed by multi-island visits from a Korean all-star team (1924), the Manila all-stars (1927), Keio University from Japan (1927), the Negro League's Philadelphia Royal Giants (1932), a Japanese all-star team (1936) and an all-star Plantation League team from the Philippines (1936).

BASE BALL

Like the passing of the ship, so goes football, for the present; and baseball looms in view. Well, the long and short of it is, that the Aggies paid for the ice cream in the indoor game, but in the outdoor game the shoe was on the other foot. In the latter there was nothing to it, as may be seen in the accompanying picture, in which Capt. Hicks' Engineers, is seen *almost* making a home run. (If the reader will examine the picture he will see the ball just entering the catcher's mit.) This is an illustration of how the Aggies won. It was suggested that each member of the engineer team be presented with a miniature baseball with which he might practice and soon learn the hang of our national pastime—Case says he wants one, too. For the Engineers perhaps the greatest mistake was Hicks. He repeatedly outshown everyone else in negative batting and fielding. Ballentyne and Case were playing good ball for the Aggies until a fair damsel happened along. After that, why they seemed to be tripping along suspended in the air—somewhat like baby elephants, you know.

Gus has had to wear glasses as a result of trying to watch two things at once. The doctor said it was the worst case of cross eyes he had ever seen. But, alas we all live to learn.

GEORGE C. BROMLEY, '20.

AGGIE-ENGINEER BASEBALL GAME

1—Poole and Ow; 2—Hicks, the star of the Engineer's team, making a hit (?); 3—Field, showing players; 4—Brash, the star pitcher, and Umpire Nick (real ump.); 5—"Georgie" Dear (class—yes?); 6—Hicks at bat (building in background is good); 7—The "Aggies" winning team: Bromley, Brash, Yung, Fuchino, Ballentyne, Kuwamoto, Pahau, Kim and Poole.

A page from the 1917 UH yearbook (*Ka Palapala*) details the heroics of the Aggies squad.

GOIN' PRO

Honolulu's Johnnie Williams was the first Hawai'i native to play in the Major Leagues. He pitched briefly for the Detroit Tigers in 1914, with six seasons more in the minors. John won nineteen games for the Western League's St. Joseph Drummers in 1916 and went 17-7 for the 1913 Sacramento Sacts of the old Pacific Coast League.

Hilo Pitcher Kenso "Wonder Boy" Nushida was the first AJA player to play in the Pacific Coast League. After years mowing down batters for Asahi, he signed with the Sacramento Senators in 1932. The Senators would change their name to the Solons and, ironically, eventually move to Hawai'i to become the Islanders.

Tony Rego (at five feet, four inches tall) was the second Hawai'i native to make it to "The Show" and the first from Maui (Maui's Shane Victorino honors Rego on his website). Tony caught briefly for the St. Louis Browns (1924–25) and spent fourteen seasons in pro ball (including several in the old Pacific Coast League for classic teams like the San Francisco Seals and Los Angeles Angels). Later, he was the first Hawai'i-born manager on the mainland, serving in the Yankee organization.

J. Ashman Beaven spearheaded the O'ahu Baseball League in 1912, and in 1925, he bought fourteen acres to build Honolulu Stadium. A true promoter, he organized the trips that brought ballplayers like Babe Ruth to the Islands. Beaven is a member of the Hawai'i Sports Hall of Fame.

Tourism was becoming big business in Hawai'i by then. At the start of the twentieth century, Waikiki Beach, with its spectacular view of Diamond Head, was always crowded with visitors from the east (the Americas) and the west (Asia). Islandball was thriving among local teams. And before long, other teams would visit Hawai'i—from both continents—to play baseball. College teams and barnstorming brigades of all-stars made their way over aboard great steamships, spearheaded by the greatest name the game has ever known.

CHAPTER 2

BARNSTORMIN' BABE

Babe Ruth slept here, played here and quenched his thirst here long before the mai tai was invented.

In the years before airlines went directly from the U.S. mainland to Asia, the giant cruise ships stopped off in Hawai'i—putting the Islands squarely dead center on the map. And since off-season ballplayers liked to supplement their incomes in those days, they'd barnstorm their exhibition games across America and beyond—way beyond. So ironically, being so far away, Hawai'i actually hosted most of the big-name Hall of Fame superstars who propelled baseball into the spotlight.

But the Bambino was hardly the first star to stop by; big-leaguers visited the Isles before Ruth was even born to further fuel Hawai'i's thirst for Cartwright's magical Island elixir.

In 1889, A.G. Spalding scheduled a world baseball tour that included Honolulu. The game was set for Makiki Field, but the ship arrived a day late and no games were allowed on Sundays, so it never happened. (Still, the players got a luau at the queen's place.)

In 1908–09, Reach Sporting Goods staged a baseball tour that included stops in Hawai'i, the Philippines, Japan and China. American ballplayers faced local squads. Manager John J. McGraw "is the barnstorming buccaneer of baseball," the *Los Angeles Times* wrote nearly a century ago. The Hall of Fame manager won eleven pennants and three World Series titles and, in the off-season, took teams of all-stars anywhere he could find a diamond (and a saloon). "He has cruised the Spanish Main and its environs,

From the seaward gazes of the locals, we can wonder if Babe Ruth's beachfront homer ball reached from Waikiki to California. *Photo by Tai Sing Loo, Bishop Museum.*

demonstrating inside baseball to those sitting in darkness and playing cricket and ukuleles," the *Times* tongue-in-cheeked. "He has invaded the Hawai'ian Islands, the Philippine Islands, Ceylon, the British Isles and Brooklyn with baseball teams."

Hall of Famer Grover Cleveland Alexander headlined a 1914 tour that played five games in Honolulu. Two squads—one from each league—played against one another before a combined team beat O'ahu's all-stars. Alex won that game 4–1 on a four-hitter.

In 1916, Pacific Coast League star Dutch Ruether brought a group of ballplayers over to face the All-Chinese all-stars, the U.S. Army's African American Twenty-fifth Regiment team and several other local squads.

Young ballplayers like Casey Stengel, who hit .368 for McGraw's 1922 World Champ Giants, would make a trip after season's end. ("I was such a dangerous hitter," Casey once quipped, "I even got intentional walks during batting practice.") Stengel became equally effective on the bench (ten pennants and seven World Series rings—including five in a row) after Joe DiMaggio made him a genius. In 1955, the Yankee skipper returned on a lengthy Pacific exhibition jaunt.

AND THEN CAME THE BABE

Yet larger-than-life Babe Ruth always got the most attention. Babe often led barnstorming teams across the country during the off-season, and he first came to Hawai'i in 1933. (Babe's entourage of all-stars was en route to Japan as part of a lengthy global tour.) The Bambino drew a crowd wherever he went—and he always loved it. He even put on a hitting exhibition from the sands of Waikiki Beach, with Diamond Head as a backdrop. He would later surf there with the biggest name in that sport, Duke Kahanamoku.

Ruth met with the governor, hobnobbed with other celebs and sold tickets to watch him play golf (he carded a 75 at the Waialae Country Club). According to legend, Ruth knocked several baseballs out of Honolulu Stadium, nicknamed the "Termite Palace" (the worst of all possible nicknames for a facility made of wood). It was relatively new then, having opened in 1926 (a rather impressive undertaking for a city that had no professional baseball team), but it would yield an extraordinary history of its own.

Babe was a bigger-than-baseball celebrity at the time and always found time for a photo op—like when he went for an ocean outrigger ride and tried his hand at surfing on Waikiki Beach with Duke Kahanamoku.

Over the decades, Honolulu Stadium also hosted football (Jackie Robinson played there for the pro Los Angeles Bulldogs in 1941), concerts (everything from Irving Berlin to Elvis) and other events of all kinds (like evangelist Billy Graham). "It creaked—actually creaked—like it was alive. Kinda spooky," said KSSK radio's Larry Price, who also played and coached there. Dave Baldwin, who pitched for the Islanders for five seasons in the '60s and '70s (before becoming a professional engineer) said, "The well-known joke was that all the termites were holding hands and that if they ever let go, the whole thing would fall apart."

Barnstorming Johnny Kerr was the first to belt a ball clear out of the yard, accomplishing that feat even before the Babe did it. Kerr was with the Hollywood Stars team of the old Pacific Coast League at the time (1927), and he also played eight seasons for the Tigers, White Sox and Senators. Ironically, he hit only six homers in the big leagues.

The stadium was torn down in 1976, and Old Stadium Park now occupies the spot at the corner of King and Isenberg Streets. Aloha Stadium (made of termite-proof steel) replaced it. Part of the old wall surrounding the stadium survived the wrecker's ball. Near the corner, there's a marker in place for the tourist who's gotten off the well-beaten Waikiki path. Appropriately, the marker uses indigenous materials: the plaque is mounted on a chunk of volcanic lava rock and includes an image of the old grandstand along with a loving tribute to the long-gone stadium.

THE BAMBINO GOES ISLAND HOPPING

After he finished touring the tiki bars on O'ahu, Babe sailed to Hilo to perform some belting exhibitions there, too. If, as the local press reported, eight thousand people greeted the entourage, that means pretty much everybody in town was on hand. Facing off against the Waiakea Pirates, Ruth delighted the crowd by pulling a pair of 450-foot homers out of the park and into a nearby pasture.

Before the game, the Babe graciously agreed to award the Hilo Baseball League's 1933 MVP trophy. The lucky recipient was Masuo "Monjou" Masutani of the Waiakea Pirates. Energized by the event, the Pirates beat the Babe (who was playing for the Hilo all-stars) 7–6.

In addition to belting homers into the stands, the Bambino also went out to Kilauea and smacked several baseballs into the volcano's smoking crater to entertain the throngs who followed his every move.

While in Hilo, Ruth was one of the first celebrities to plant a banyan tree along Banyan Drive. The wooden marker in front of Babe's banyan marks the date he dug in: October 26, 1933. It's gotten a bit taller since then, and like Ruth himself, Babe's banyan grew nearly as wide as it did high. Banyan Drive, located along the way from the airport into town, developed into a significant sightseeing spot for Hilo. Over the years, more than fifty luminaries have dug in the fertile volcanic dirt here, including Cecil B. DeMille, King George V (Queen Elizabeth's pop), Franklin D. Roosevelt and Amelia

FINAL EDITION

HILO TRIBUNE HERALD

A DAILY NEWSPAPER FOR THE ISLAND OF HAWAII

SUGAR REPORT 3.30

VOL. XI Member of the Associated Press — HILO, HAWAII, SATURDAY, OCTOBER 28, 1933 — Price 5 Cents — NO. 251

THOUSANDS TURN OUT TO WELCOME 'KING OF SWAT' ON HILO VISIT

WORLD NEWS

(Associated Press by Wireless)

Deny Rumor Of Army Officers' Execution

MEXICO CITY, Oct. 28 (AP)—Rumors that several army officers were executed for an alleged plot to seize control of the army was denied officially today.

Denials came from the war department, an dthe Santiago military prison where two officers were known to have been arrested and 18 more were reported incommunicado.

Graf Zeppelin Cruises Over Capitol Buildings

WASHINGTON, Oct. 28 (AP)—The Graf Zeppelin arrived here at 1:35 p. m. and cruised over the capitol and the White House.

AKRON, Oct. 28 (AP)—The Graf Zeppelin took off for Germany at 8:55 a. m. today.

Pope Is Anxious Over German Youth

VATICAN CITY, Oct. 28 (AP)—The Pope expressed himself as "deeply preoccupied and acutely anxious over the situation of the Catholic youth in Germany, especially for the religion of Germany."

The pontiff made the statement Friday to a pilgrimage of German youths.

Guard Called To Halt Strike Mob

COLUMBIA, S. C., Oct. 28 (AP)—

HAWAII NOT INCLUDED IN RETAIL CODE

Deputy Will Work Out Code for Territory Upon His Arrival In Hawaii

Dole Announces Coffee Code Now Considered Includes Islands In Provisions

WASHINGTON, Oct. 28 (Special)—The final retail code draft does not apply to Hawaii, NRA officials explaining that a deputy will be charged with the duty of working out the Hawaii retail code along the same lines as continental codes when he arrives there.

Dan McGregor, former assistant secretary to Victor Houston, will serve as secretary to ... the latter announced today.

WASHINGTON, Oct. 28 (AP)—James Dole, chief of the food processing division, said today that the coffee code under consideration ... Hawaii which will be allowed to make certain exceptions because of local conditions.

The code in its present form provides a 40 hour week and 40 cents minimum hourly pay for men and 37½ cents for women. The

THE BABE RUTH FAMILY

Babe Ruth and his family were given a rousing ovation upon their arrival here this morning. They are from the left, Miss Julia Ruth, the Babe himself, and Mrs. Ruth.

INTERCEPTOR TO BE CONSTRUCTED

Public Works Fund Boost Is Now Considered

AUTHORITY TO HANDLE FUND

NATIONAL HERO OF BASEBALL IS GIVEN SILVER KEY TO CITY

Babe Ruth Arrives for Local Exhibition At Hoolulu Park; 3000 Crowd Pier with Thousands of Others Lining Streets to Catch Glimpse of Visitor

Reception is Held At Mooheau Park Pavilion Where City's Welcome is Extended by Chairman Spencer, Big Banquet is Planned for Tonight

George Herman (Babe) Ruth, "King of Swat," arrived in Hilo this morning and was warmly received by 8,000 people. Mrs. Ruth, Miss Julia Ruth, Don Watson, sports editor of the Star-Bulletin, and Red McQueen of the Advertiser sports staff were also in the Ruth party.

They are here to help boost Babe in his local exhibition at Hoolulu park Sunday afternoon, and also for a bit of sight-seeing. Babe's stay will be short—he is sailing ... but he and his family hope to see all there is to see in the way of scenery before leaving the Big Island.

A throng estimated at 3,000 crowded the pier when the S. S. Hualalai docked and at least 4,000 more lined the streets of the town, giving Ruth one of the warmest welcomes ever accorded a visitor to these shores.

Met Off Port

Ruth and his party were met off port by a reception committee representing the Hilo Baseball league. The committee rode out into the harbor on a launch and boarded the Hualalai.

On the committee were T. E. M. Osorio, president of the Hilo Baseball league, Alfred Jasinth, ...

RELIEF PLEDGED TO BUS GROUP BY LEGISLATORS

Compromise Measure to Be Introduced At Legislature On Bus Question

Pledging support to the Hilo Bus association in its fight against the payment of high rates of public liability and property damage insurance ...

Above: The Babe and his brigade invaded the Big Island, too.

Right: Babe Ruth and Monjou Masutani in Hilo, 1933.

Left: Babe Ruth practicing horticulture on the Big Island in 1933.

Below: Some 1934 Connie Mack All-Stars in Hawaiʻi. *Back row, left to right*: Lou Gehrig, Pinky Higgins, Lefty Gomez, Babe Ruth, Jimmie Foxx, Earl Averill, Al Simmons, umpire John Quinn and Moe Berg (who did some prewar spying on the Japan leg of the tour, filming sites around Tokyo for the U.S. government; Ruth chose to gather data about the *sake* establishments instead). *Front row, left to right*: Bill Dickey, Frank Crosetti, Charlie Gehringer, Lefty O'Doul, Earl Whitehill, Mickey Cochrane and Lefty Grove.

Earhart. Besides FDR, another future U.S. president is represented: Richard Nixon. In a checkered irony, Nixon's plant was accidentally erased (washed out to sea, anyhow) by a tropical storm on the same day he was elected vice president in 1952. Fortunately, Mrs. Nixon came out in her plain Republican coat and replanted the tree (as well as one for herself) when Watergate was getting out of control. But hers also mysteriously vanished (along with eighteen and a half minutes of her husband's executive ordermaking back in Washington).

The Bambino brought Yankee teammate Lou Gehrig along when he came back in 1934. As he did everywhere he played, Gehrig amazed locals with his mighty blasts. Connie Mack and Ruth were leading an all-star team to Hawai'i and Japan that year. Mack created the Philadelphia Athletics in 1901 and led them to five World Series wins. But he stuck around way too long, forcing his A's into the cellar for decades before finally retiring after 1950. In Honolulu, Mack's squad beat the Hawai'ian Baseball League all-stars 8–1. The Bambino hit two doubles, and Gehrig whacked a homer out of Honolulu Stadium.

Lefty O'Doul, who had hit .398 in 1929, made the trip to the Isles with his bride, Jean, in 1934 (the record does not show whether she referred to him as "Lefty" or "Francis"). The O'Douls would stop in Honolulu many more times after the war. They also leied over en route to Asia with the newly married Mr. and Mrs. Joe DiMaggio, twenty seasons on in 1954. Jean was a close friend of Marilyn Monroe and accompanied the star frequently.

Mr. and Mrs. Francis O'Doul after just having landed at Māmala Bay, 1934. The couple posed in front of the famed Aloha Tower, which would be riddled with bullets seven years later during the attack on Pearl Harbor.

Around the time Babe and his buddies were visiting the Isles, O'ahu native Henry "Prince" Oana was getting a cup of coffee at "The Show." Henry played in six games for the Phillies in 1934 and came back up as a pitcher for the 1943 and 1945 Detroit Tigers. Along the way, he was a star in the minors. During a twenty-three-season career, Prince racked up 261 homers and a lifetime .304 average. He also pitched well, winning twenty-four games one season, and managed in the minors for four years. In Hawai'i, his fame achieved heroic proportions.

Native son Prince Oana.

Southpaw Clarence Kumalae pitched in the friendly confines of Chicago's Wrigley Field.

Lesser known was Hawai'ian Clarence Kumalae, who actually suited up with a major-league team a year before Oana did. Clare got a tryout with William Wrigley's Los Angeles Angels of the old Pacific Coast League in 1933 and earned a spot on the semipro Catalina Cubs, as well as being a batting-practice pitcher for the parent club. He also pitched for Omaha and Cedar Rapids in the Western League and won eleven ballgames with Vancouver in 1937. Kumalae spent the bulk of his pro pitching seasons with the Wrigley organization in Catalina, Los Angeles and Chicago but never did "officially" make the big-league roster.

A group from Hawai'i barnstormed over to the mainland in 1935. The all-Hawai'i squad scheduled 150 games over the spring and summer and selected local players from the Islands. There were ringers, though; Johnny Kerr, who'd played eight seasons in the majors, was listed as a pitcher from the all-Chinese team.

In 1936, the House of David team barnstormed over to Hawai'i. John Hubbell, the

Charlie and Dorothy Root wave bon voyage with daughter Della and Charlie Jr.

younger brother of New York Giants Hall of Famer Carl Hubbell, made the trip. He performed well enough on the Isles to earn a tryout with the Giants the following spring. But he never quite mastered the screwball like Carl did, and he played six seasons in the minors without ever pitching in "The Show."

Other players simply passed through. After the 1932 World Series against the Yankees, Chicago Cub pitcher Charlie Root took his family on a multi-month cruise to Australia and other exotic ports; Hawai'i made for a nice stopover.

Baseball celebrated its official centennial in 1939, with plenty of barnstorming still coming to the Islands. Ruth made another trip, along with plenty of mainland all-stars. But the trade winds of war were blowing, and Hawai'i's world was about to change again.

CHAPTER 3

World War II and Joltin' Joe

While the war interrupted the barnstorming ballplayer tours, it hardly put a dent in the superstar steam that flowed into Hawai'i. Actually, World War II further fueled the big-name parade into the Pacific, as plenty of the era's biggest ballpark heroes not only played there but were also stationed there. Included in that group was Joltin' Joe DiMaggio, who wowed local crowds with his mighty blasts.

Those Pacific-based units all had their own teams that played against one another. The army and navy fielded formidable squads featuring DiMaggio and fellow Hall of Famers Pee Wee Reese, Red Ruffing, Joe Gordon and many others.

Transport ships, rather than airplanes, brought the boys over from the West Coast of the mainland. (Gerry Priddy, DiMag, Dario Lodigiani, Mike McCormick and Walt Judnich made the trip over to Hawai'i together.) Since they rode trains for long road trips to ballgames back home in those days, they were used to playing cards and pulling pranks to pass the time.

Sammy Hairston is noteworthy. In 1951, he became the first African American to play for the Chicago White Sox, and his sons (Jerry and Johnny) and grandsons (Jerry and Scott) have also played in the big leagues. But in 1944, neither Major League Baseball nor the U.S. military were integrated yet (Hairston was still playing in the Negro Leagues), so the handpicked Seventh AAF bent a few rules to get him on the squad in already integrated Hawai'ian baseball.

The integrated Seventh AAF team included Joe DiMaggio and Sammy Hairston.

DiMaggio, of course, was the star of the show. By the time he entered the service, he'd already been MVP twice and had five World Series rings for the Yankees. He was an army PR man's dream addition to the Hawai'ian diamond, and he did not disappoint. Several DiMag homers flew out of Honolulu Stadium. His first went 435 feet, and fans said it was the longest ever hit on the Islands. And forget boat lag—Joe pulled that feat the day after he arrived in June 1944, much to the delight of twenty-six thousand screaming fans.

Joe's Seventh AAF team won twenty-eight straight ballgames to handily take the Hawai'i Baseball League crown, decimating other military teams, local amateur squads and college clubs along the way. (They'd been 3-4 before DiMag and his wrecking-crew buddies arrived.) They then swept the aptly named Cartwright Series (three more wins in a row) before heading to the Central Pacific Area "World" Series. And that's where Army collided with Navy—whose manager, Bill Dickey, fielded a team that included Reese, Schoolboy Rowe, Johnny Mize, Johnny VanderMeer, Scooter Rizzuto, Bronc Broncato, Hugh Casey, Virgil "Fire" Trucks, Kenny Sears, Joe Grace and a Boston Red Sox kid named Dominic DiMaggio.

Unfortunately for the Army boys, Joltin' Joe didn't play (stomach trouble), Ruffing had a sore arm, and Priddy had been transferred. The Blue team whipped the Green team in four straight to win the pennant. Joe Grace blasted a grand slam for Navy in one of those contests. Grace played for the St. Louis Browns and Washington Senators on the mainland and the Pearl Harbor Submarine Base while at sea.

Above: DiMaggio blasts one out of the Termite Palace.

Right: Future Hall of Famer Pee Wee Reese (Chief Specialist Harold Reese to his draft board) played for the Aiea Naval Hospital team. He faced off again Joltin' Joe (army air force sergeant Joseph P. DiMaggio) at the Central Pacific Area Service Championship on July 7, 1944. Here, the boys polish some brass before the ballgame.

The service teams played plenty of their exhibition games at Honolulu Stadium. These games were used as fundraisers for the War Bond effort and attracted large crowds. To sit in the reserved section, you had to buy a $50 bond. Fans lined up to get scorecards, balls and scraps of paper autographed by the players. Before the games, bats and balls were auctioned off to raise even more funds. They brought in more than $500,000—quite a sum in the '40s, a time when DiMag had yet to make $50,000 in a single season.

The local press played up the local angle, posing the great Sergeant DiMaggio with some local produce.

Guys who just happened to be stationed there got to play against their heroes. Teams like the Kaneohe Klippers, the 3,177th Signal Corps Company (known as "Happy Pappy's Playboys," giving a nod to their manager, Captain Pappy Starnes) and the 184th Infantry Regiment of the 7th Infantry Division (stationed

BRIG. GEN. William J. "Bill" Flood (left), 7th AAF Chief of Staff and sponsor of the finest ball club ever to play to civilian audiences in Hawaii. Top star Joe DiMaggio (center)—7th AAF photos. Lt. (jg) Bill Dickey (right), manager of Navy CPA champions.—U.S. Navy photo.

Big League Baseball in Hawaii

By CARL MACHADO

Bill Flood, we thank you! That is the sentiment of the many thousands of baseball fans who have flocked to the Honolulu Stadium—there were as many as 26,000 at each of several games—to watch Brigadier General William J. "Bill" Flood's great 7th AAF ball club perform in the Hawaii Baseball League.

You may well ask, "Why thank the General for fielding a ball club in the Hawaii League? There were other clubs in the League too."

Here's the reason. The sporting General, 7th AAF Chief of Staff, not only fielded a baseball club, but he gave us a club headed by none other than Jolting Joe DiMaggio, greatest ball player in the world today. The General was out to give Hawaii the best ball club possible—and he did it. It is a safe bet Honolulu baseball fans would never have had the opportunity to see a real big league club perform if it had not been for the impartial sportsmanship of Bill Flood.

The Hawaii League for 1944 was under way, with the 7th AAF's "B" team taking four beatings, winning three, when Jolting Joe & Company arrived. Then things began to pop—in favor of the Bombers.

With the Yankee Clipper came Mike McCormick, Cincinnati Reds; Walt Judnich, St. Louis Browns; Dario Lodigiani, Chicago White Sox; Ferris Fain and Al Lien, San Francisco Seals; Bill Schmidt, Sacramento Solons; Rugger Ardezoia, Kansas City Blues; Gerald Priddy, Washington Senators; Bob Dillinger, Toledo Mud Hens; Charlie Silvera, Wellsville; Carl De Rose, Amsterdam; Bill Leonard, Oakland Acorns of the Pacific Coast League. Lt. John T. (Long Tom) Winsett, team manager, was formerly with the Brooklyn Dodgers.

When the announcement was made that Joe DiMaggio would show at the stadium on Sunday, June 4, only one day after arriving here, the fans went wild. A flock of over 26,000, the greatest throng in Hawaii League history, turned out to see what they expected to be only a two-inning courtesy showing of the Yankee Bomber.

JOE "FLASH" GORDON lives up to his name in Stadium practice.—7th AAF photo.

No one expected Joe to play the whole game—he had just come in and hadn't seen a baseball for six weeks. But when the game started, there was DiMaggio at his customary Yankee post in center field. But this time he proudly displayed the letters "7th AAF" on his chest. Yes, General Flood had him out there to give the fans a run for their money.

The great DiMag proceeded to demonstrate to Honolulu ball fans — civilian and service—the reason he is the greatest attraction in baseball. Three times the Clipper came to the plate, but didn't do much with the shillelah, but the fans were satisfied for Joe had played magnificent ball out in the field. However, the crowd and the General wanted to see a DiMaggio home run, and Joe wasn't going to disappoint them.

Came the ninth, and DiMaggio strode to the plate, to powder the ball over the left field fence, into Dreier Manor. The ball travelled 435 feet, by actual measurement. Only one other player had ever accomplished that feat in the twenty years of baseballing at the stadium, and that was our own Johnny Kerr, now a member of the U. S. Coast Guard. However, Joe did the trick in his first game—Kerr played many years for his.

Inside that same edition of *Hawai'i* magazine, readers learned about other All-Stars on the Isle (like Bill Dickey and Flash Gordon, pictured) and saw Sewin' Joe DiMaggio at work on his own government-issue threads.

at Schofield Barracks) got clobbered by the 7th AAF, but they didn't mind—their families back home got autographed baseballs in the mail. And everybody wanted to play; the Coast Guard team had enough ballplayers that it could split into two for intrasquad games at multiple locations. Besides staging ballgames at the Termite Palace across town, the military teams could also play at Furlong

A 1944 poster leveraged Sergeant DiMaggio's presence at an upcoming ballgame out on Maui.

Field (at Pearl Harbor), among other stops.

The guys received official recognition for their efforts—Islandball equivalents of MVP trophies and World Series rings. Soldiers and sailors were awarded Certificates of Merit for taking part, and if a Brownie camera was nearby, scrapbooks at home filled up with images of dads and uncles and sons posing next to their back-home baseball idols.

Taking a page from barnstorming Babe Ruth, the Seventh AAF went to other islands to clobber competitors, too. DiMag and his buddies also belted long balls in Maui to the delight of even more loyal fans and played a pair of games on the Big Island at Hilo's Hoolulu Park (winning 5–2 and 5–0, with six thousand fans overflowing the creaky grandstand). The Army all-stars and Navy all-stars also came to Hilo a few months later, battling to a 6–6 tie in fourteen innings (without Joe, who'd already shipped back stateside to his native California).

The championships extended to teams on islands beyond Hawai'i. Joe Garagiola played for the Manila Dodgers (named by player-manager Kirby Higbe) before returning to the Cardinals organization and ultimately embarking on his broadcasting career.

Bob Borkowski actually got his major-league contract as a result of being stationed in Hawai'i while a fresh-from-school teenager. "I was with the navy," Bob recalls, "and I took care of the infield. Billy Herman was the manager. I asked him if I could pitch batting practice, and he

Mr. and Mrs. Joseph DiMaggio, honeymooning in Hawai'i. This time, Joe flew, and when they landed, Mrs. D. apparently was popular enough to get leied more than once.

asked if I could get it over the plate. I did that for a few days, and it turns out one umpire's dad was a scout for the Cubs. So they signed me up as a pitcher—no bonus, no nothing!" Back in the States, Bob won eighteen as a rookie for a team with a very non-military-sounding name (the Elizabethton Betsy Cubs)—but he also hit .384, with power aplenty, so they converted him to an outfielder. Bob ended up playing six seasons in the majors for the Cubbies, Reds and Brooklyn Dodgers.

Some of the ballplayers were so taken with Hawai'i that they returned after the war. In 1954, Joe DiMaggio and his new bride, the former Norma Jeane Dougherty, stopped over as part of their Asian honeymoon.

CHAPTER 4

Postwar Baseball

After life got back to normal, the barnstorming tours to the Far East resumed. Some of the names and faces were new, but the lineups were still star studded.

Major-league teams (from as far away as New York City), minor-league teams and still more all-star squads braved the journey to Hawai'i, waving their way through welcome parades before heading to the ol' ballpark to ply their trade. The locals loved it, the press ate it up and the boys delighted in doing their thing in paradise.

Just a few months after the war ended, in the fall of 1945, Chuck Dressen led a team of National League All-Stars to the Pacific. Dressen, then a Brooklyn Dodgers coach, chalked up a 17-5 record in Hawai'i, the Philippines, Guam and other South Pacific islands.

In 1946, the Harlem Globetrotters basketball troupe came to Hawai'i. Its owner, Abe Saperstein, also had a Negro League baseball all-star team (the Cincinnati Crescents). So, he brought his baseball club over, too, along with Olympic Gold Medalist Jesse Owens, who raced a local horse before the game. (The horse came from behind for the win.) They performed in both Honolulu and Hilo.

That same year, the Brooklyn Dodgers sponsored a "Brooklyn Against the World" contest; winners from all forty-eight states, Canada and U.S. territories (like Hawai'i) would travel to Ebbets Field to play some baseball and watch exhibitions between George Sisler's All-Stars and Leo Durocher's

Brooklyn Eagles. The winning Island teen was Henry Tominaga, a pitcher who'd just graduated from Honolulu's McKinley High.

Lefty O'Doul led postwar healing to Asia. In the midst of his twenty-three-season managerial career in the Pacific Coast League, the San Francisco Seals skipper took teams to Japan, stopping in Hawai‘i (his initial layover as a '30s All-Star). He also brought his Seals to Honolulu for spring training (1946) and Maui (1947), where they went 20-2 against locals.

In 1948, a group of Hawai‘ian all-stars (including Crispin Mancao, who would later pitch for the Hawai‘i Islanders, and Jimmy Wasa, an AJA legend) joined the regrouped Harlem Globetrotters baseball team (now a squad of West Coast Negro Baseball League players) to barnstorm on the mainland. They played seventy-nine games in hallowed locales like Chicago's Wrigley Field and Yankee Stadium in New York, where they drew a crowd of twenty thousand.

Joltin' Joe liked to frequent Hawai‘i, often joining his buddy O'Doul for exhibitions against local and Japanese teams. In 1951, Joe brought brother Dom back, along with Billy Martin and others, but they lost to a military all-star squad 8–6.

The next winter, DiMag remembered that Phillies ace Robin Roberts had held him to one hit in the 1950 World Series, so he brought Roberts along to hold the military barrage down. Other past World Series notables came along as well, including Enos Slaughter and Yogi Berra, and traveled to Kaua‘i and Maui while there. Joe relaxed a bit more in '53, providing some photo ops for the paparazzi of the day. One afternoon, as the cameras clicked away, he even took the time to demonstrate the ancient sport of surfing to Joe Jr. in the gentle waves off Waikiki Beach.

Tokyo's College All-Stars played some games in Honolulu and Hilo in 1950, and the Yomiuri Giants stopped by in 1953, led by Hawai‘i hero Wally Yonamine.

The New York Giants also swept by in '53, with Leo Durocher at the helm. (During the Japan leg of the trip, Leo was coaching first base and, rather loudly, told the runner to run on the next pitch. But catcher Jyun Hirota gunned him down; Lippy didn't know that Hirota had attended the University of Hawai‘i and had understood every word!)

The following winter, Eddie Lopat brought his off-season all-stars for some exhibitions, and Yonamine brought his own all-star team over from the other direction.

Other all-star teams played in Hawai‘i all through the 1950s. In '55, the Yankees (spearheaded by Whitey Ford) and Brooklyn Dodgers (headlined

Above: Joe DiMaggio surfin' with his son at Waikiki, 1953.

Right: Mickey Mantle (top left), Billy Martin (top right) and Yogi Berra (bottom) in the tropics.

Casey Stengel hammed it up in Honolulu—just like he did everywhere else.

by Duke Snider) orchestrated a six-week tour of Hawai'i (O'ahu, Kaua'i and the Big Island), Japan, the Philippines and Guam. This was right after the World Series, in which the Brooks had actually defeated the Yanks, so interest was sky high.

Yanks Mickey Mantle and Billy Martin enjoyed the opportunity to drink in the local atmosphere. Yankees catcher Yogi Berra played there, too, perhaps butchering the Hawai'ian language as much as he did English. But the boys brought their stuff to the local diamonds, winning 12–1 at the Termite Palace and 22–2 at Hoolulu Park in Hilo. Casey Stengel led the brigade and butchered English alongside Berra—returning triumphantly for another Pacific barnstorming trip.

During the winter after the 1956 regular season, the entire Brooklyn Dodgers squad played two games in Honolulu (and one in Kahului, Maui) en route to their Japan tour.

In the late '50s, after Yonamine's successes, more all-stars visited Hawai'i from the East (which we suppose is their West, actually). The Tokyo Giants played some baseball in Honolulu as well.

A pair of Tokyo Giants visiting paradise.

Stan Musial came to Hawai'i and gave clinics to kids (on both O'ahu and the Big Island) in 1965, two years after he'd retired. Hundreds of youngsters showed up for the events, sponsored in part by the local Little League groups.

MOWIN' 'EM DOWN IN MANOA

When Les Murakami arrived to coach baseball at the University of Hawai'i at Manoa in 1971, it was an intramural sport—no intercollegiate competition. He had no scholarships to offer, but no matter—there was no equipment, either. And no field! Undeterred, Les built an NCAA Division I powerhouse. Over the next thirty seasons, his teams went to the NCAA tournament eleven times. The Rainbow Warriors were ranked number one in the nation in 1979, and his 1980 squad finished second nationally. Les won 1,079 ballgames and sent seventy-six players on to play professional baseball. His honors include being a two-time Hawai'i Sportsman of the Year, a Lefty Gomez Award winner, District Coach of the Year and Western Athletic Conference Coach of the Year (twice). Les is in two halls of fame: the American Baseball Coaches Association Hall of Fame and the Hawai'i Sports Hall of Fame.

Eleven of Murakami's student-athletes made the majors: Chuck Crim (class of '82), Glenn Braggs ('83), Joey Meyer ('83), Chuck Jackson ('84), Mike Campbell ('85), Bruce Walton ('85), Larry Gonzales ('88), Scott Karl ('92), Mark Johnson ('96), Jay Spurgeon ('97) and Dusty Bergman ('99). Braggs won a World Series ring with the 1990 Reds (after playing against the Islanders in Honolulu in '86 while with Vancouver in the PCL), and a

UH legend Les Murakami.

twelfth UH alum, Steven Wright ('06), reached the majors after Coach Murakami retired.

Mike Trapasso took over as head coach in 2002. (He'd pitched in the Cards and Braves systems in the '80s). After more than a decade at the helm, Coach Trap has won more than three hundred ballgames for the still-winning school.

In all, 112 UH ballplayers have played at the pro level—so far.

CHAPTER 5

The Islanders

Hawai'i hosted numerous homegrown amateur teams over the decades but finally joined the ranks of official organized baseball in 1961. The Hawai'i Islanders, newest member of the fabled Pacific Coast League, meant the Isles were now just a step away from the Major Leagues.

Before they washed back ashore to the mainland in 1987, the Islanders provided plenty of Island thrills and let the locals see plenty of future big-leaguers (as well as a good number of former major-league players still hanging on) right here in Honolulu.

The Sacramento Solons were a longtime component of the old Pacific Coast League, first suiting up in 1918. Utah native Nick Morgan Jr. bought the franchise and moved it to Honolulu for the 1961 season, creating the westernmost team in organized baseball history. The *Honolulu Star-Bulletin* staged a naming contest; the 247 entries included creative approaches like "Poi Dogs" and "Da Guys." Management settled on renaming the club the Hawai'i Islanders, and professional baseball was finally "official" on the Islands—thanks to the advent of air travel.

The team was the Triple A affiliate of the Kansas City A's, and being just one step from the Major Leagues meant players would occasionally get the call and shuffle up to the big club. Of the forty-one ballplayers who appeared on the Islanders roster during the course of the season, twenty-seven played in the majors at one time or another. Overall, the team finished a semi-dismal 68-86 under a pair of managers: Tommy Heath and Bill Werle. And the arrangement with Kansas City ended after one year, before the

Honolulu and vicinity: Partly cloudy tonight and Saturday. Few isolated showers. Moderate trades. Temperatures last 24 hours: High 82; low, 71. .04 rainfall

Honolulu Star-Bulletin

HONOLULU, HAWAII, FRIDAY, APRIL 21, 1961

Honolulu Star-Bulletin, Vol. 50, No. 111 ★★★★ HOME EDITION 10¢

Honolulu Gets First Look At Its New Baseball Team

Mayor Blaisdell and Governor Quinn "opened" the PCL season last night as pitcher and catcher before the professionals took over. — Star-Bulletin photos.

Colorful Isle Program Marks Pre-Game Show

A program of international flavor marked the pre-game activities for last night's inaugural of Pacific Coast League baseball in Honolulu.

Starting at 6 p.m. when less than 200 fans were in the stands, the program ran until 7:45. Musical entertainment was provided by the Royal Hawaiian Band, Aurora Flores, Filipina songstress, the Halla Huhm Korean Dance Studio, a trio from the Hanayagi Dancing Academy, and also included a lion dance by the Chinese Physical Culture Society, and solos by Haunani Kahalewai and Jimmy Moikeha.

Mayor Neal S. Blaisdell and Governor William F. Quinn formed the "battery" for the pre-game plate ceremonies. Both were a bit wild, Blaisdell on his tosses to the plate, Quinn on his relays to the mound.

Phillip Snodgrass, a Little Leaguer, the batter, got to swing only two "good" pitches. Dan Lau, Honolulu police chief, was the umpire and got only a little beef from Governor Quinn.

A view of the crowd attending Hawaii's first professional baseball game. They saw the Islanders beat Vancouver 4 to 3. (Story in Sports Section)—Star-Bulletin Photo.

The natives greeted their new ballclub with the same level of enthusiasm that Babe Ruth received all those years before.

team began longer affiliations with the Los Angeles Angels and Washington Senators, among others.

Early on, the idea was to play some home games on other islands, but on the very first flight to Maui, the plane had serious engine trouble and was forced to make an emergency landing. So that idea was scrapped—after they'd already made it to a game in Hilo, on the Big Island, whipping Spokane 11–2 for a June crowd of nearly two thousand.

Half a century after the Wasada University team began playing in Hawai'i, Waseda alum Akihito Kondo played in Honolulu. To celebrate the Islanders' inaugural season, the team played some exhibition games against Japan's reigning champs. In fact, the diminutive Konda (all five feet, six inches of him) had been MVP of the Nippon Series (Japan's version of the World Series) in 1960. Kondo later managed in Japan, including at Chiba Lotte from 1997 to 1998 (in between Islander alum Bobby Valentine's tenures).

And it was never dull. The fabled Hollywood Stars had tried cheerleaders in the same Pacific Coast League in the '50s, so the Islanders figured they could give "usherettes" a try. The Islanders held spring training in San Bernardino, California, in 1962—for reasons we cannot fathom—and a group of local businessmen (headed by Chinn Ho) bought controlling interest in the team in 1963.

MANAGERIAL TALENT

Tommy Heath was the Islanders' first manager, but he lasted only until August. Tommy caught for the St. Louis Browns from 1935 to 1938 and managed in the minors for eighteen seasons (1947–64) before becoming a scout for the Angels. Heath had plenty of PCL experience, heading the San Francisco Seals from 1952 to 1955, the Sacramento Solons (1956–57) and the Portland Beavers (1958–60). He won one title, with Trenton, in 1948.

Bill Werle was named interim manager midway through the Islanders' first campaign, but he didn't return the next spring. He later managed in Hawai‘i, this time against the locals with the Giants' PCL club. Bill had pitched for the Pirates, Cards and Red Sox from 1949 to 1954 and for five teams in fourteen years in the Coast League (including a stint for Hawai‘i in '61, when he was forty). His nickname was Bugs because…he liked bugs. So the first-year Hawai‘i Islanders finished sixth out of eight teams, holding onto the spot they'd taken their final year over in Sacramento.

Irv Noren came aboard as skipper for the 1962 and 1963 seasons as the Los Angeles Angels became the Islanders' parent club. Irv had just completed an eleven-season career in the majors (he was an All-Star in 1954, hitting .319 as the Yankees starting right fielder next to Mickey Mantle) and was a part-time player-manager for Hawai‘i. He led the team to back-to-back winning campaigns: 77-76 and 81-77.

Hub Kittle became the Islander GM (1962) after playing/managing wartime Hawai‘iball. His eight-decade career is legend: 144 wins pitching (1937–58), over 1,000 wins managing and a 1982 World Series ring (Cards coach). At age fifty-two (1969), Hub pitched two innings for Savannah. At fifty-six (1973), he closed an Astros-Tigers exhibition, earning the save for manager Leo Durocher. And at sixty-three (1980), Hub pitched a scoreless inning for Springfield. "The sucker bunts," Hub growled, "so I knocked him down!"

Hall of Famer Bob Lemon replaced Noren in 1964 (to a dismal 60-98), several seasons before managing in the Major Leagues, where he did much better—guiding the Yanks to the 1978 World Championship). Yet it wasn't Lemon's first baseball trip to the Isles. While in the navy in 1945, Bob was stationed at the Aiea Barracks. He'd briefly played in the majors before the war as an infielder, but while in Hawai‘i, he switched to pitching (and ended up winning twenty games seven times for Cleveland). Ironically, when baseball returned to Sacramento in 1974, Lemon was the Solons' first manager, guiding his squad's away games back in Honolulu.

Lemon was succeeded by George Case, who oversaw two seasons (75-72 in 1965 and 63-84 in '66) as the Islanders became the top farm for the Washington Senators. A four-time All-Star, he'd played for the Senators and Indians from 1937 to 1947, leading the majors in steals five straight years. George won the College World Series while coaching at Rutgers. He also managed and coached in the minors and coached for the Senators from 1961 to 1963.

Wayne Terwilliger guided the Islanders to a 60-87 last-place finish in 1967. Well into the twenty-first century, Twig was the last remaining major-leaguer from the 1940s still suiting up. He broke in with the Cubs in 1949, played in the majors over the course of three decades (teammates with Jackie Robinson and Willie Mays) and has coached and managed in the majors and minors ever since. As a big-league coach, he was part of Ted Williams's staff in Washington and won World Series rings with the Twins in 1987 and 1991. After managing the St. Paul Saints for several seasons, he's been coaching there since 2005. The 2010 season marked his eighth decade in professional baseball.

Bill Adair managed the Islanders to a solid 78-69 mark in 1968 (the first of the club's two lone-season affiliations with the Chicago White Sox) and an even 73-73 in '71 (the squad's first year with the San Diego Padres). Bill played twenty-one years in the minors (1935–56) but never made the majors. He hit 182 home runs and had a lifetime batting average of .291. He also managed twenty-one years—twenty in the minors (1949–73) and part of one (ten games) for the 1970 White Sox, where he went 4-6 between Don Gutteridge and Chuck Tanner. Alas, he was the best of the bunch, as the Pale Hose finished 56-106. Adair also coached at the big-league level for the Braves (1962 and 1966), ChiSox (1970) and Expos (1976). His clubs won 1,611 games (for a .552 clip) and six pennants.

Chuck Tanner took over for two seasons, 1969 (74-72) and 1970, when the club returned to the Angels' organization. Chuck brought the Islanders their first-ever championship that second year (98-48). That team was named thirty-eight Greatest Minor League Team of All Time by MiLB.com. Chuck played eight years in the majors, and his performance in Hawai'i earned him the White Sox top job. He managed twenty-nine years in the big leagues, winning the 1979 World Series with Pittsburgh.

Jimmie Reese served as an Islanders coach under Tanner. Jimmie's career pretty much spanned the entire twentieth century, as he was involved with professional baseball over the course of nine decades. He roomed with Babe Ruth's suitcase and was still coaching in the majors in the '90s. He broke in as the batboy for the Los Angeles Angels in the old Pacific Coast League in 1919, first played for the Angels in 1920 and finished up with them in 1940 (putting in three seasons with the Yanks and Cards in between) before beginning his managing/coaching/scouting career. Reese was manager of the San Diego Padres against the Islanders for Hawai'i's inaugural 1961 season and finished up as a hitting coach for the California Angels—a position he held until he died at the age of ninety-two, in 1994. The Angels retired his uniform number (fifty), and he's in the Pacific Coast League Hall of Fame.

Rocky Bridges held the helm in 1972 (74-74) and kicked off 1973, at which time the club was firmly entrenched in the Padres' system. He ultimately managed in the minors for twenty-one years (1964–89, 1,381 wins), leading the Phoenix Giants (against the Islanders) from 1974 to 1982 and winning the East Division in '77. Rocky came back to the PCL to head Vancouver in the Islanders' final season, 1987, and coached seven seasons for the Giants and Angels. A 1958 All-Star for Washington, he played eleven years in "The Show," breaking in with Brooklyn in 1951.

Warren Hacker pinch-managed in the middle of the tumultuous 1973 season; he was one of three managers that year. (Roy Hartsfield mopped up to a 70-74 final mark.) Warren pitched in the majors for twelve seasons and had some previous Islandball experience: he had spent several springs pitching for the Chicago Cubs on Catalina Island back when the team held its pre-season drills off the Southern California coast.

Hartsfield stayed around for a while and in 1975 led the Islanders to their second pennant. (They were 67-77 in '74, avoiding the cellar, thanks to the new Sacramento Solons). Hartsfield played briefly for the Boston Braves and also managed the Toronto Blue Jays. In all, he managed seventeen seasons in the minors, four of them in Honolulu. He also managed at the 1975 Pacific Coast League All-Star Game, held at Hughes Stadium in Sacramento, on his way to an 88-56 record and the Western Division title. Roy's boys also won the West in 1976, when they went 77-68.

Hartsfield was succeeded by Dick Phillips, who'd played for the Islanders in the '60s. Phillips was a veteran utility man, playing first, second and outfield from 1965 to 1967 after a brief career with the Giants and Senators. He headed Hawai'i from 1977 to 1979. He started strong, placing first in the PCL Western Division and second overall in '77 (79-67) but didn't fare as well after that, going from first to worst in 1978 (56-82) and ending 1979 with a 72-76 mark.

Doug Rader managed the Islanders for three seasons (1980–82) before managing the Rangers, White Sox and Angels. He finished above .500 all three

Dick Phillips, who'd later manage the team, models the Islanders' home flannels at the Termite Palace in 1966.

years in Honolulu (76-65 in 1980, then 72-65 in '81, winning the North Division, and 74-70 in 1982).

Rader was succeeded by Tom Trebelhorn, whose '83 team finished one win above .500 (72-71) during his only season at the helm. That year marked the first year for Hawai'i as a Pittsburgh Pirates farm team. Trebelhorn played five years in the minors, managed the Brewers and Cubs, coached for the Orioles and Cubs and managed twelve years in the minors, including a season in Honolulu as the Portland skipper (1982) and with North Division champ Vancouver (1985). Italy named him its National Team coach for 2009.

Tommy Sandt led Hawai'i from 1984 to 1986, during which time the Islanders won the South Division in 1984 (87-53) and 1985 (84-59) but lost in the playoffs both times. The team tumbled to 65-79 in 1986. Sandt had played briefly for the A's and finished his career with the Islanders, going one-for-two as a pinch-hitter in '74. As a coach for the 1997 Florida Marlins, he was part of a World Championship team.

After Sandt left, Bob Bailey managed the team for its final season, 1987, taking the team to a ninth-place finish (65-75) during its second one-year stint with the White Sox. Bailey had played in the majors from 1962 to 1979, hitting over twenty homers three times, and had previously managed six seasons in the minors.

Bobby Valentine didn't manage the Islanders, but he did play for the team before managing the Rangers, Mets, Red Sox and Chiba Lotte Marines in Japan. His 2000 Mets won the National League pennant. As

He'd Love Hawaii

ONTARIO, Calif—Outfielder Charley Secrest, recently assigned to Shreveport, certainly would have fallen in love with Hawaii for one reason—no snakes. The fleet-footed flychaser breaks any and all records in "getting away" when a snake crosses his path, or when he crosses a snake's path.

Borsch

This applies to all snakes, large or small, harmful or harmless, dead or alive.

The subject of snakes came up for discussion in an early evening bull session. One of the players was attempting to convince Charley that sidewinders abound in this part of the California country.

Charley, not quite knowing whether to believe the "snake expert," paled a bit and finally said:

"At least I'll know what to do if I see one—run like blazes!"

Secrest also feels the "running urge" come on strong when such critturs as tarantulas and scorpions crawl into sight.

"Those tarantulas are ugly things," Charley shuddered. "They are nothing but big, black spiders with monkey hair on 'em." He shuddered again.

In his rookie days Charley played ball in the southwest where snakes, tarantulas and scorpions thrive. One day, so the story goes, he broke (unofficially) the high jump record for baseball parks.

"I was legging out an infield grounder and after crossing first base I almost stepped on a big snake rolled up in the dust," Charley recalled.

Ferd Borsch covered every Islanders home game through the team's entire 1961–87 run. His friendly style entertained and informed *Honolulu Advertiser* readers for more than forty years.

a ballplayer, he hit .306 for Hawai'i in 1976, earning a promotion to the parent Padres.

Visiting managers brought some excitement along, too. Before he joined the Dodgers coaching staff and ultimately became skipper himself, Tommy Lasorda managed the Spokane Indians and Albuquerque Dukes in Honolulu.

UP IN THE BOOTH

Despite their far-off location, the Islanders managed to seat some pretty significant names in their broadcast booths over the seasons.

Harry Kalas was elected to baseball's Hall of Fame in 2002 after announcing Phillies games for thirty-nine years. He was also the voice of NFL Films and the Islanders' first announcer (1961–64). Mainland flights were costly, so Kalas "re-created" road games from KGU-760 studios (KOHO-1170 presented games in Japanese). "If I had something to do," he said, "games would finish in one hour and fifteen minutes. Guys would swing at the first pitch."

The Islanders broadcast booth was filled with other future celebrities. Hank Greenwald took over in 1965, and he stayed for three seasons. After getting back to the mainland, Greenwald did radio and TV work for the Giants, Yankees and A's. Marty Chase worked the booth from 1966 to 1968 (after helping Kalas in '64), and Dick Phillips moved from the field to the booth to assist Chase in 1968 (before managing the club in the '70s).

Not long after Al Michaels graduated from college, he got his first broadcasting job as the Islanders' radioman in 1968. He, too, had to re-create road games. Al also called games for the University of Hawai'i and was named Hawai'i Sportscaster of the Year in 1969. While on O'ahu, he also appeared in an episode of *Hawai'i Five-0*. "I had about seven lines that got edited down to two when the show aired," Al recalls. "Never got an Emmy nomination, though."

Al got help from Chuck Leahey in 1969 and Ken Wilson in 1970. When Michaels left, Wilson stuck around to add color for Les Keiter from 1971 to 1972.

Keiter called the games from 1971 to 1975 and 1978 to 1983. Before he came to the Islands, Les had been in New York and Philadelphia, where he worked all the major sports and also covered boxing and the Olympics. He

Long before we all knew him, Al Michaels entertained the locals in Hawai'i.

was with KHON-TV and, like Al, was on *Hawai'i Five-0*—but Les made more than one appearance. Keiter often played top military brass, earning the nickname "General." He's in both the Hawai'i Sports Hall of Fame and the National Baseball Hall of Fame. In fact, Keiter's career was so successful in so many directions that he got to write an autobiography about it all. Don Robbs acted as Keiter's color man in 1973, and Dave Oishi also filled the airwaves in 1974.

From 1976 to 1977, Jim Leahey and Mel Proctor were the team. Allan Elconin joined Keiter from 1979 to 1980, and Jack Wiers manned the booth from 1984 to 1986, ably assisted by Leahy for two years and then by Keiter. The final crew, in 1987, consisted of John DeMoss, Keiter and Tom Yoshida.

OTHER HAPPENINGS AT THE OL' TROPICAL BALLPARK

Occasionally, an interesting beyond-baseball event would break out at the palace. In 1972, it was an on-field fire—apparently the grounds crew thought igniting some petrol would help dry the rain-soaked infield.

But the highlight of the 1972 campaign was even better: pitcher Ralph Garcia married fiancée Terri Rivas on the mound in between halves of a double-header against Tucson. Manager Rocky Bridges gave the bride away, Dick Baney came in from the bullpen to serve as the best man and outfielder Lee Maye sang a song. About twelve thousand of the couple's closest friends attended.

The big Aloha Stadium (top) and little Murakami Stadium (bottom).

During their first fifteen seasons, the Islanders hosted home games at Honolulu Stadium. But its "Termite Palace" nickname was a little too true, so the team moved to brand-new, cavernous Aloha Stadium across town. Aloha's seating capacity is fifty thousand—a vast increase. Mackay Yanagisawa played a pivotal role in the facility's development. After managing Honolulu Stadium for twenty years, Mackay was an Islanders part owner and then managed Aloha Stadium. He founded the Hula Bowl (1947) and the Aloha Bowl and played a key role in bringing the NFL Pro Bowl to Hawai'i.

The team played some home games at Les Murakami Stadium during its last two seasons, 1986–87. This ballpark, with its dramatic view of Diamond Head, was built in 1984 on the University of Hawai'i campus for UH games. The Rainbow Warriors still play there, and after the Islanders moved away, the Hawai'i Winter Baseball League began playing there, too. Its seating capacity is 4,312—great for college ball and certainly not too cavernous (like Aloha Stadium), yet not enough to sustain a Triple A franchise.

But interest waned, and oftentimes there were more termites than fans; attendance plummeted from a peak of 467,217 in 1970 to never topping even 150,000 during the '80s (despite guys like Tony Gwynn and Barry Bonds populating the rosters). The club was losing more than a quarter of a million dollars a year in its final few seasons.

The boredom became so rampant that the press barely covered the team's final game in 1987; the brief in the *Honolulu Star-Bulletin* (a tiny, one-column tidbit) doesn't even bother to mention the club's name in the headline ("AAA team: Aloha")! At least the guys won (10–4), beating Vancouver overseas in Canada. Pitcher Joel McKeon got the last win,

More termites than fans…local lore held that the (human) crowds were often so sparse that you could literally hear the (insect) crowds chomping away on the bleachers below.

and Daryl Boston smacked a two-run homer in the sixth to put Hawai'i ahead—for the final time. (Their last home game, a loss, had been seen by only 3,819 die-hard fans.)

Islander owner David Elmore pulled up stakes after the 1987 season, moving the team to the mainland—where it became the Colorado Springs Sky Sox (he'd also considered Portland and Salt Lake City, two old PCL cities that were also teamless at the moment). The Sox were then part of the Cleveland Indians organization for five years and have been the top farm club for the Colorado Rockies ever since. The club plays at non-poetically named Security Service Field. At the time, Elmore tossed a bone to the few remaining fans by pledging to move a Class-A team to Hawai'i to continue the Hawai'i Islanders name. But that never materialized.

LOCAL TALENT MAKING GOOD

In all, eight Hawai'i-born players had suited up for their home team. Pitcher Crispin Mancao was the first, taking the mound in the inaugural 1961 season at the age of forty-three (and the height of five feet, four inches). The following year, Bill Nishita also tossed a few games. Then Andy Miyamoto played some outfield in 1965, followed by Aran Ahu (1974), Kala Kaaihue (1975 and 1977, when he hit .314 in limited service before serving as bullpen catcher in 1987) and Derek Tatsuno (1986–87).

None of these guys made it to "The Show," but a pair of other local products played for the Islanders and also made the majors. The first was John Matias, although he ironically got it backward: he played for the Chicago White Sox in 1970 and then the Islanders in 1972, 1973 and 1980. Fred Kuhaulua also played in the majors ('77 Angels) before Hawai'i (1979–82). So, strangely enough, no Hawai'i-born ballplayers ever played for the Islanders on their way up to "The Show."

CHAPTER 6

SINCE THEN

While the Islanders' departure in 1987 closed one chapter of baseball in Hawai'i, the game—as it always has—played merrily on. The University of Hawai'i continues to wallop opponents near and far, other minor-league clubs got going and lots of other happenings kept things interesting. The key item: On April 19–20, 1997, the San Diego Padres and St. Louis Cardinals played a three-game series at Aloha Stadium. These were regular-season major-league games—not exhibitions—the first official big-league games ever held in Hawai'i. The Cards won the opener, 1–0, and game two of the double-header, 2–1. San Diego's bats woke up for game three as the Padres cruised to an 8–2 victory (presented live on ESPN) with 40,050 attending. Royce Clayton got the first-ever base hit in Hawai'i, and Ron Gant hit the first (and so far, only) homer.

Beyond that, native Hawai'ians continue to make it to the majors—representing almost all the six major Isles (Little Lāna'i is still working on it). Like the DiMaggios, the Sardinhas produced a band of three brothers in the baseball business, all of them having wowed the crowds at Honolulu's Kamehameha High. Bronson was the first Hawai'ian-born million-dollar bonus baby, and his middle name contains enough syllables for plenty of nicknaming opportunities: Kiheimahanaomauiakeo.

One star who almost made the majors was Glenn Goya. Pitching for Punahou, Glenn twirled a perfect game against St. Louis High to win the 1972 Hawai'i State Championship. He went on to become the first Island native to win an NCAA batting title—Glenn tallied an impressive .485

average for Colorado State in 1977 while also pitching for the Rams. He had an impressive rookie season at Great Falls the following year (.324) and did well at Fresno (.299) before getting a tryout with the Islanders. But some early injuries took their toll, and he had to retire at the age of twenty-five. CSU named Glenn to its hall of fame in 1999.

In 1973, Major League Baseball commissioner Bowie Kuhn said he could envision the possibility of an international league with a Pacific division, including teams from Honolulu, Japan and the West Coast. (Kuhn was equally successful in presiding over important baseball issues like the Curt Flood situation, the first players' strike and the early use of performance-enhancing chemicals.)

The First Hawai'ian Bank branch near the main university campus is a museum to the island's sports heritage. This office is directly across the street from the old ballpark site, and of course the venerable bank was founded by Alexander Cartwright. Before you even enter, the tour begins: the windows feature a baseball diamond design. Inside, several displays house memorabilia from the Islanders, the Plantation Leagues, AJA and other ethnic teams and more. A massive two- to three-story wall exhibit celebrates the events that took place at Honolulu Stadium. The lobby is also home to

A First Hawai'ian Bank branch also acts as a miniature museum to Hawai'iball.

There's another Hawai'i baseball history display at the Honolulu Airport.

the state high school baseball championship trophy. And from the second-story balcony, you can gaze through another baseball-diamond window to view Moilili Field, to the north.

Next time you're in Honolulu's airport, you can visit the displays for Maui-born Wally Yonamine. Wally has two display cases, since he played pro baseball and pro football (as a San Francisco 49er, he was the first Japanese American in the NFL). He achieved his greatest success playing baseball in Japan—an eleven-time all-star. (Check out more about Wally at the end of the next chapter).

Few artifacts remain of Hawai'i's baseball past beyond those locations, although a few pieces populate private collections. Local baseball historian Nelson Okino guards plenty of Hawai'i's baseball past, like Chuck Hartenstein's Islanders jersey from the early '80s.

The Hawai'i Winter Baseball League brought professional baseball back to the Islands in 1993 with the Hilo Stars, Honolulu Sharks, Kaua'i Emeralds, Maui Sting Rays, Waikiki Beach Boys, West O'ahu Cane Fires and North Shore Honu. A few other teams cropped up, too: the Kaneohe Bay Dawgs, Kona Man-O-Wars and Lahaina Whalers.

Some locals did well: Kala Ka'aihue (Sharks) smacked nearly one hundred homers in the mainland minors, brother Kila has enjoyed a couple cups of

Chuck Hartenstein's game-worn Islanders jersey.

Kona with Kansas City and papa Kala had played seven seasons in the minors (the last two with the Islanders).

The league lasted five seasons, folding after the 1997 campaign, and staged a three-year comeback from 2006 to 2008. In all, nearly one hundred HWBL players made the majors at one time or another.

Ichiro Suzuki played for the Hilo Stars in the inaugural season. In fact, Ichiro hit .311 and was named the league's first MVP, leading his squad to the pennant. Also that year, Jason Giambi (Kaua'i) batted .343—two seasons before being named the American League MVP with the A's. Others who stopped by include hometown hero Benny Agbayani, A.J. Pierzynski, Aaron Boone, Buster Posey, Craig Counsell, Derrek Lee, Gabe Kappler, Mark Kotsay, Quinton McCracken, Shane Spencer and Todd Helton.

Two women played in the Hawai'i Winter Baseball League: first-baseperson Julie Croteau and pitcher Lee Anne Ketchum, on loan from the Colorado Silver Bullets in 1995. They were the first women to play in a Major League Baseball–sanctioned league, and Julie was the first to get a base hit. Croteau went on to manage the USA Women's National Team and win the Women's World Cup.

Lots of Little Leaguers on the Isles have earned themselves trips to Williamsport. In 1988, Pearl City took second in the world, and the Ewa Beach Little League team won the 2005 World Championship. In 2008, Waipahu took the title, and in 2010, they came in second. Despite Hawai'i's size, only six U.S. states have won more Little League World Series crowns.

Julie Croteau played pro hardball in Hawai'i.

But there's more. Little League is for eleven- to twelve-year-olds; the Junior League World Series (players aged thirteen to fifteen) has also heard some noise from Hawai'i. Pearl City won that title in 1984, while Aiea won back-to-back crows in 2000–01. Pearl City came back to take all the marbles in 2007, and in 2008, the Hilo squad was the runner-up. At this level, only Florida has more titles (five). Hawai'i and California are tied for second with four each.

Little League's Senior League (ages fourteen to sixteen) has seen its share of championship Island clubs, too. Hilo has taken the title twice (in 2003 and 2011), and Pearl City grabbed back-to-back silver medals in 2005–06.

But Hawai'i's first international youth baseball championship came in 1969, when Honolulu's PAL Americans won the PONY League (ages thirteen to fourteen) World Series. The team from Kahului, Maui, also won the championship in 1980. In other PONY Divisions, the 1979 squad from the same Honolulu PAL won the Colt League (ages fifteen to sixteen) crown in 1979, and Hilo took the title in 1989. In the Bronco League (ages eleven to twelve), Maui won in 2001 and Ewa Beach in 2010.

A Honolulu team won the American Legion National Tournament in 1980. Moiliili Legion Baseball manager Clyde Hayashida and coach Ronald Jacobs shared the legion's Jack Williams Memorial Leadership Award that year for their efforts.

The Hawai'i High School Athletic Association's annual baseball finals are called the Wally Yonamine Foundation Baseball Championships, in honor of the local hero. Baldwin High fielded the first champs in 1959. The games split by school size in 2008 to form two divisions.

A team called the Hawai'i Island Movers, a squad of local college stars that plays in the summertime, has been touring the state (and Asia) since 1984.

And of course, the AJA Baseball League—now more than one hundred years at play—continues to support numerous teams across the Island chain, culminating in the crowing of a champion at its annual tournament. The highlight of the league's legendary exploits may be its 5–3 upset of 1974 World Champion Cuba in front of twenty-five thousand fans in Tokyo. (The Japanese Cultural Center of Hawai'i guards this rich tradition with exhibits and a treasure-trove of artifacts and photos.)

Back to the pros. In 2010, the Golden Baseball League started a team in Wailuku, Maui—the Na Koa Ikaika ("Strong Men")—and that league was swallowed up by the North American Baseball League, which added a team in Hilo (the Hawai'i Stars) before folding two seasons later. But hope springs eternal in paradise, and both Hawai'ian teams have been included in the start-up Pacific Association of Professional Baseball Clubs.

Since Then

The Maui club plays at Maehara Stadium, adjacent to War Memorial Stadium in Maui's sports complex. (College football's all-star game, the Hula Bowl, was played at War Memorial Stadium from 1998 to 2005). The baseball park was named after Ichiro "Iron" Maehara, a Plantation League alum who went on to scout for the Dodgers for decades, signing Sid Fernandez, among others.

Hilo

Besides Babe Ruth's visits, Hilo's baseball history contains plenty of other interesting items. The main stomping ground is Francis Wong Stadium, named after a local who heavily supported youth athletic programs. Over the years, a few of the all-star teams dropped by from their Honolulu visits. Hall of Famers like Joe DiMaggio, Casey Stengel, Yogi Berra, Mickey Mantle and Stan Musial performed their magical feats on the Big Island, too.

Francis Wong Stadium, Hilo.

A 1939 statue inside Wong Stadium celebrates Alexander Cartwright and the centennial of his inventing the game.

Wong Stadium, which opened in 1971 and reflected the fancy architecture of the time, replaced Hoolulu Park in the same location. It played host to the Hilo Stars of the Hawai'i Winter Baseball League and the Hawai'i Stars of their various leagues, and it's still the home field for college ball and plenty of other games. Inside the ballpark's main entrance, there's a stone marker honoring Honolulu's own Alexander Cartwright. The inscription reveals that the marker was created by the Hilo Senior Baseball League in 1939.

CHAPTER 7

The Ballplayers

Between Hawai'i natives who made it to the majors and mainland warriors who played regularly on the Isles, plenty of recognizable names share significant links to playing in paradise. Just over three dozen Hawai'i-born ballplayers have made it to the majors so far—quite a collection, as seen here. And a cast of thousands played for (and against) the Islanders during their twenty-seven-year Pacific Coast League tenure, a passing parade that included a few big stars. Following are a few of the most interesting ones.

Benny Agbayani

Honolulu-born Benny Agbayani played ball at Hawai'i Pacific University (after playing for St. Louis High School, where he also wowed local crowds in football and soccer). He spent a few seasons starting in the Mets' outfield (knocking in a couple runs in the 2000 World Series) and wore number fifty in honor of his homeland. Agbayani also played six seasons in Japan (managed by his old New York skipper, Islanders alum Bobby Valentine) until he was thirty-seven and was named MVP of the first Asia Series (in 2005).

Benny borrowed an idea from a Hawai‘i Islanders game by getting married at home plate of the 1998 Triple A All-Star Game (wearing a Hawai‘ian shirt, of course). He's in the Hawai‘i Sports Hall of Fame, and these days he's back on O‘ahu, helping kids at Mililani High. Benny is one of seven baseball players on the *Sports Illustrated*/CNN 1999 list of "The 50 Greatest Hawai‘i Sports Figures," coming in at number thirty-six.

Hank Allen

Hank Allen was an Islanders star in 1966, hitting .299 with twenty-three homers. He played in the majors from 1966 to 1973 for the Senators, Brewers and White Sox. Hank finished up in Hawai‘i in 1974, playing a partial season. His brothers Richie and Ron also played in the majors. After retiring, Hank became a successful Thoroughbred trainer, reaching the Kentucky Derby.

Brant Alyea

Garrabrant Alyea, a mainstay in Honolulu from 1965 to 1966, was a starting outfielder and sometimes first-baseman who hit twenty-seven homers at the age of twenty-one. He played six seasons in the bigs (1965–72) for the Senators, Twins, A's and Cardinals. Brant smacked a homer on the first major-league pitch he saw and won a World Series ring with the '72 A's. His same-named son played in the minors from 1985 to 1990.

Bobby Balcena

Bobby Balcena was the first Asian in the Major Leagues. Balcena inauspiciously broke a racial barrier ten seasons after Jackie Robinson did it more famously, playing seven games for the 1956 Cincinnati Redlegs. (In 1965, Masanori Murakami would become the first Asian-born big-league player.) Bobby was born in the United States in 1925 in a Filipino fishing community in California. His pro career spanned the years 1949–62. Balcena started the Islanders' inaugural season, 1961, with Vancouver (a Pacific Coast League rival, playing some early away games in Honolulu Stadium) before joining the Islanders. He also played with Hawai‘i in '62. In all, Balcena swatted 134 homers in the minors while also legging out ninety triples.

Dave Baldwin

Dave Baldwin was a rare submarine pitcher, plying his trade for the Senators, Brewers and White Sox from 1966 to 1973. A setup man and closer, he finished with a solid 3.08 career ERA. He spent five of his fourteen minor-league seasons in Hawai'i (1965–66, 1971–72 and 1974), plus another year pitching away games there (1970) for Portland. He won a total of twenty games for the Islanders.

Bo Belinsky

Bo Belinsky became famous for throwing a no-hitter in his fourth start as a rookie (for the LA Angels) in 1962. He then became infamous for gallivanting all around Southern California, dating plenty of movie stars. He somehow managed to bounce back and forth to the majors for eight seasons (Angels to Philly to Houston to Pittsburgh to Cincy), getting his final shot at "The Show" in 1970. (He won only three games after 1965.) On one of his many rehab assignments, he also pitched a no-hitter for the Hawai'i Islanders in 1968. Bo pitched well all three of his seasons in Hawai'i (1963, 1968 and 1969), striking out 181 in 176 innings in '68 and going 12-5 with a nice 2.82 ERA in '69.

Rafael Belliard

Rafael Belliard was a regular infielder on the 1985 Islanders team. He played from 1982 to 1998 in the majors (for Pittsburgh and Atlanta)—a shortstop on those dominant Braves teams of the '90s (he hit .375 in the '91 World Series and got a ring in '95). Known for his great glove, the five-foot-six speedster hit just two homers during those seventeen seasons. He coached in Atlanta for years and now coaches for Detroit.

Dennis Bennett

Dennis Bennett went 18-8 for the 1970 championship Islanders after winning thirteen in '69. He led the club in wins both years and was twice named a PCL all-star. He also pitched for Hawai'i in 1972 and 1973 after playing away games there for Tacoma (1968) and Salt Lake City (1971–72). He put in seven seasons (1962–68) for the Phillies, Red Sox, Mets and California Angels. He won twelve for the '64 Phils; that year, his brother Dave pitched his only inning in the majors—closing a game that Dennis had started.

Carlos Bernier

Carlos Bernier is the only Hawai'i Islanders player in the Pacific Coast League Hall of Fame. He played sixteen years in the minors, eleven of those in the PCL for the Hollywood Stars, Salt Lake Bees and Hawai'i. Carlos was a charter Islander in '61 and one of the few to play four years for the team. The first year, he hit .351 with twenty homers. In 1962, he hit .313 with seventeen dingers. In '63, he hit .300 and twenty-six home runs. And in 1964, he had twenty-seven more round-trippers and a .294 average. He led the Coast League in steals three times (65 in 1952), finishing with 408 Coast League swipes and exactly two hundred minor-league home runs. Carlos spent most of 1953 with the Pittsburgh Pirates.

Mike Bielecki

Baseball America named Hawai'i Islander Mike Bielecki its 1984 Minor League Player of the Year. Mike set a team record with nineteen wins (against just three losses). But go figure: he was back in Honolulu the next season instead of in Pittsburgh. When he finally hit the bigs, he lasted fourteen years, during which time he had one 18-7 season (1989) for the Cubs and three no-hit innings during the 1996 World Series for Atlanta. Since he broke in at age nineteen in the minors in 1979, Mike's pro playing career spanned three decades—a rare and impressive feat.

Ethan Blackaby

Ethan Blackaby finished his nine-year minor-league career with the 1969 Islanders—previously playing road contests in Honolulu for league opponents from Denver (1963–64), Salt Lake City (1965), Oklahoma City (1967), and Seattle (1968). He'd gotten cups of coffee with the Milwaukee Braves in 1962 and '64. After retiring, he was general manager of the Phoenix Giants from 1974 to 1985—facing Hawai'i a couple hundred times during a PCL career that spanned nearly the Islanders' complete lifespan.

Barry Bonds

The most famous (and infamous) of the Bonds brigade played in Hawai'i. Barry was with the 1986 Islanders (back when he was thin) and hit .311 with seven dingers in 148 at-bats. Barry played seven seasons for the Pirates

(1986–92) and then fifteen with San Francisco (1993–2007). He was named the National League MVP seven times. Clearly, his accomplishments are asterisk-laden to many fans and most sportswriters—who pledge to never vote for him to enter the Hall of Fame.

Bobby Bonds

Barry's slightly less-famous dad played in Hawai'i during away games when he was with the 1968 Phoenix Giants. Bobby hit .370 that year, earning his ticket to the big club in San Francisco, where he started a fourteen-year major-league career that resulted in three All-Star Game appearances, three Gold Gloves and three seasons in which he led the National League in strikeouts. He hit a grand slam in his first major-league at-bat. Over the course of his career, Bobby became only the second ballplayer (alongside Willie Mays) to hit three hundred homers and swipe three hundred bags.

Bobby Bonds Jr.

Bobby Bonds Jr. played for the Hilo Stars during the Hawai'i Winter Baseball League's inaugural season, 1993, and later for the Honolulu Sharks. In all, Bobby played eleven seasons in the minors but never made it to "The Show." He started off good, hitting .317 for the Rookie League Padres in the 1992 Arizona League, but couldn't maintain that level. Junior did hit .317 for the San Jose Giants in 1997, and he smacked a career total of sixty-two homers.

Dick Bosman

Dick Bosman pitched a no-hitter against the defending World Champ A's in 1974. His career spanned eleven seasons (1966–76), splitting time with the Senators/Rangers, Indians and A's. He paced the American League in 1969 with his 2.19 ERA, going 14-5. Dick was an ace for the 1967 Islanders, winning twelve with a 2.76 ERA. He coached in the minors for years and also in the majors for the White Sox, Orioles and Rangers.

Daryl Boston

Daryl Boston stopped by in 1987 to play twenty-one games for the final-season Islanders—smacking the team's final homer. He roamed the outfield for the White Sox, Mets, Rockies and Yankees from 1984 to 1994. His brother D.J. played sixteen seasons in the minors. Daryl coached in the minors for several years, and these days, he's the ChiSox first-base coach.

Clete Boyer

Clete Boyer was a Gold Glove third baseman for sixteen seasons (1955–71) for the Kansas City Athletics, Yankees and Atlanta Braves. He timed his stay with the Yankees well—Clete got to play in five straight World Series, winning two rings. Before heading off to play four seasons in Japan, Clete manned the hot corner for Hawai'i in 1971—a thirty-four-year-old vet among the youngsters. His brothers Ken and Cloyd also made the majors, and four other brothers played in the minors. His son Mickey and one nephew also played pro ball. Clete later coached for the A's and Yanks.

Angel Bravo

Angel Bravo was a consistent hitter (.281, .279) for the Islanders in 1968 and 1972, bookending his 1969–71 big-league career with the White Sox, Reds and Padres. He got to play in the 1970 World Series with the Big Red Machine. Angel played ten years in the minors, visiting Honolulu for away games with Indy (1967) and Tucson (1969), and then toiled five seasons more in Mexican League outfields. He also played eighteen winters in his native Venezuela.

Kenneth Bray

For decades, Father Kenneth Bray coached baseball—and influenced lives—at the Iolani School. Before he passed away in 1953, he had coached numerous other sports for the Raiders, too. The school itself got its start in 1863, with help from King Kamehameha IV and Queen Emma, and its alumni roster includes Sun Yat-Sen. Father Bray was one of the earliest members of the Hawai'i Sports Hall of Fame.

Marshall Bridges

Marshall Bridges was quite the character. Bridges won a World Series ring with the 1962 Yankees (despite serving up the first grand slam in series history, to the Giants' Chuck Hiller). He was the last remaining Sacramento Solon to play for Hawai'i, finishing with the Islanders in 1967. And in 1963, a lady in a bar shot him in the leg during spring training.

Bridges broke in with the Memphis Red Sox of the Negro Leagues before the New York Giants offered him a contract in 1953. He made it to the majors with the Cardinals in 1959 (on the same staff as future Hall of Famer Bob Gibson) and also pitched for the Reds and Senators through 1965. He finished 1965 on the Nats' farm, in Hawai'i, where he went 2-0 with a perfect 0.00 ERA in five games. The following year, he was 2-2 with a still-nifty 2.53 ERA, closing forty-eight games.

George Brunet

George Brunet's career spanned the ages. "Lefty" pitched three decades in the majors, and after he "retired," he started out as a thirty-eight-year-old rookie in the Mexican League (where he pitched twelve more seasons until he was just shy of fifty). George is the all-time minor-league strikeout king (3,175 over thirty-three seasons) and has another 921 at "The Show"—more than 4,000 whiffs in all. George won 313 games in pro baseball and holds the Mexican League record for shutouts, with fifty-five. He was elected to the *Salon de la Fama* (the Mexican Baseball Hall of Fame) in 1999. In all, Brunet pitched for thirty professional baseball teams (nine in the majors, fifteen in the minors and six in ol' Méjico). Along the way, he pitched for the Islanders for two seasons; in 1972, he was the ace, going 14-9.

Doug Capilla

Known for his blazing fastball, Honolulu-born Doug Capilla pitched for the Kaulua High Surfriders. Signed by the Giants, he played for the Cards, Reds and Cubs from 1976 to 1981. Doug started out in the minors in 1970; as a teen rookie, he whiffed 69 in just 38 innings and in his second season fanned 192 batters in a mere 161 frames.

Bob Chance

Bob Chance was with the Indians, Senators and California Angels between 1963 and 1969. He played three straight seasons for Honolulu (1965–67), hitting .294 in '65...and won the Eastern League Triple Crown in 1963 (26 homers, 114 RBI, .343). He also played Islandball in Japan and Puerto Rico. Bob's son Tony played twenty seasons in the minors, hitting 202 homers, but never made it to "The Show."

Joe Charboneau

Joe Charboneau didn't make a lot of waves as a Hawai'i Islander, playing in just fifteen uneventful games in 1984, but he is included here for being a noteworthy chap in his time. Joe was the consummate flash in the pan, the very essence of the sophomore jinx. The AL Rookie of the Year for Cleveland in 1980 (twenty-three homers and a .289 average), he belly-flopped in '81 and didn't do much better in '82. And that was that. He was also a media darling in his day, famous for antics like pulling off bottle caps with his teeth and a series of other progressively more repugnant circus feats that are better left untouched here. He also appeared as a ballplayer in *The Natural* (alongside Robert Redford) in 1984, managed briefly in the minors (a career 0-5 record) and in 2000—at the age of forty-five—staged a one-game comeback for the Canton Crocodiles of the independent Frontier League. (To Joe's credit, he went one for one, batting 1.000 for a final minor-league career mark of .312.)

Tom Cheney

Tom Cheney owns a record that doubles as a trivia-quiz masterpiece. Can you name the pitcher who struck out the most batters in a single game? Nope—not Koufax, Nolan Ryan or the Rocket, but Mr. Cheney. In 1962, Tom whiffed twenty-one Orioles in a sixteen-inning contest against his Senators. But how fast we can fall—six days later, he gave up two homers to Mickey Mantle to suffer the loss. Tom also pitched for the Cards and Pirates over eight big-league seasons, having won a World Series ring with that upstart Bucs team in 1960. Cheney finished his career with the Islanders in 1966, trying to rehab after arm trouble. He didn't quite light up the stat book in Honolulu, though; Tom went hitless in just one at-bat, but he did strike out five batters in seven innings.

Jim Coates

Jim Coates pitched in three straight World Series for the Yankees (1960–62, winning two rings) and in plenty of ballgames in Honolulu after that. He was a solid member of the Islanders' staff from 1969 to 1970, finally retiring at age thirty-seven after playing away games there the previous six seasons (with Seattle and San Diego). In all, Jim won 142 ballgames during his fifteen minor-league seasons, a career that had started in 1952. He led the American League in winning percentage (.813, a 13-3 record) in '60 en route to the All-Star team. His grandson, pitcher Aaron Pribanic, is working his way up in the Pirates' organization.

Steve Cooke

Born in Kaua'i, Steve Cooke spent most of the '90s pitching for Pittsburgh before finishing up with Cincy in 1998. He started off hot, going 2-0 and then winning ten ballgames in 1993 (Topps named Steve to its All-Star Rookie Team that year), but developed arm trouble and never quite reached his rookie form. He's part of the family that founded Castle & Cooke in 1851, helping propel Hawai'i's economic growth through tourism and the agricultural business.

Pat Corrales

Pat Corrales caught for the 1974 Islanders after his ten-year major-league career. He'd primarily been Johnny Bench's backup for the Big Red Machine, and he played in the 1970 World Series. Pat later managed the Rangers, Phillies and Indians—the first Mexican American manager in the majors. Corrales won a World Series ring as a coach for the 1995 Braves, and today he's coaching for the Nationals.

Pat Corrales.

Chuck Cottier

Chuck Cottier was a slick-fielding second-baseman in the majors from 1959 to 1969 with the Milwaukee Braves, Tigers, Senators and California Angels. Amidst all that, he spent plenty of time in Honolulu. Chuck was with the Islanders from 1965 to 1966 and returned for away games during the next two seasons with Seattle and Portland. From there, he began his second career—managing. Cottier led teams in the minors for five seasons before heading the Seattle Mariners from 1984 to 1985. He's also coached for the Mets, Cubs, Orioles and Phillies. He currently scouts for the Yankees.

Casey Cox

Casey Cox was the ace of the 1969 Senators staff, twirling a 2.78 ERA for a 12-7 mark. From 1966 to 1973, he played for that franchise (into Texas) and with the Yankees. He spent part of 1965 and 1967 with Hawai'i, going a hard-luck 0-2 despite a solid 3.20 ERA—all in relief.

Chuck Crim

Chuck Crim was an All-American at the University of Hawai'i–Manoa before becoming one of the top middle-relievers in the majors. He led the American League in appearances (70/76) for the Brewers in 1988–89) and was in the bigs for eight seasons overall (later pitching for the Angels and, finally, the Cubs in 1994). He also played back in Honolulu against the Islanders while visiting with Vancouver. After retiring, he coached high school ball in California and scouted for the Dodgers. Crim was named the Dodgers' bullpen coach for 2013.

Tim Cullen

Tim Cullen blossomed in his second season for the Islanders, hitting .295 with punch (twenty-seven doubles) in 1966. The slick-fielding utility infielder earned a midseason promotion to the Senators, where he won a spot on the Topps All-Star Rookie Team. Cullen spent the next seven years in the majors, getting a World Series ring with the '72 A's. Since then, he's been a vice-president for the Fresno Grizzlies.

Ron Darling

Honolulu native Ron Darling won 136 big-league ballgames, including a 17-9 for the '88 Mets. He was a 1985 All-Star and a 1989 Gold Glove winner, and he earned a World Series ring in 1990. (He'd won one game, posted a 1.53 ERA and whiffed a dozen BoSox in seventeen innings during the '86 Fall Classic.) Ron also pitched for the A's and Expos in a big-league career that lasted from 1983 to 1995.

Ron graduated from Yale, where he once pitched eleven innings of no-hit ball—an NCAA record. These days, he's the color man for Mets games. And he can do it all in a variety of languages; Ron speaks Chinese (his mother is Hawai'ian and Chinese) and French (his dad is French Canadian). His brother Eddie played a few seasons in the minors.

Bob Davis

Bob Davis spent three years in Honolulu, batting .329 for the 1975 Islanders to earn a spot on the PCL all-star squad (see the photo on page 113). He played eight seasons in the bigs, catching capably for the parent Padres, Blue Jays and Angels.

Trench Davis

Trench Davis has such a cool name that he has no need for a nickname. He's one of the best remembered Islanders, since he spent four seasons there, played more recently than not (1983–86) and played well (53 steals in 1984 and a .311 average in '86). He swiped 283 bags during eight minor-league seasons. In the majors, Trench barely got to smell the coffee, playing in just twenty-three games over three seasons (1985–87) for Pittsburgh and Atlanta (and in sixteen of those games, he was a pinch runner). He wrapped up his pro career by running fast over the course of five more years in Mexico.

Jose DeLeon

Jose DeLeon put in thirteen years in the majors. He pitched for five teams from 1983 to 1995, and his best seasons were in St. Louis, where he won thirteen in 1988 and sixteen in '89. In fact, Jose led the loop with 201 whiffs in 1989, but we must report that he also led the league in losses in both 1985 (nineteen) and 1990 (nineteen again)—a workhorse for bad teams. He fared better in Hawai'i (twenty wins over three seasons, 1983 and 1985–86), also pitching away games there in 1982 while with Portland. In '83, Jose whiffed 128 batters in 127⅓ innings for the Islanders.

Joe DeSa

The first Damien Memorial School alum to make it to "The Show," Honolulu native Joe DeSa saw action with the Cardinals in 1980 and the White Sox in 1985, when he whacked a pair of home runs (including a grand slam) in just forty-four at-bats. (In ten minor-league seasons, mostly at top-level Triple A, he logged more than one hundred homers.) Known for his trademark thick black moustache, Joe was also a football star in high school, attracting scholarship offers from UH, among others. But while playing winter-league ball in Puerto Rico in 1986, he died in an auto accident. The Islanders honored the local hero with "Joe DeSa Day" during a game the following year. Joe's younger brother Gary (also a Damien Monarch) signed a pro contract and played a couple seasons in the minors as well, and his nephew John Matias played for the White Sox one season.

Carlos Diaz

Born in the Honolulu suburb of Kaneohe, Carlos Diaz pitched for a trio of National League teams in the '80s: the Braves, Mets and Dodgers (on a Tommy Lasorda staff that included Fernando Valenzuela and Orel Hershiser). He was a potent force from the bullpen, striking out a lot of batters and finishing up with a nice 3.21 ERA. In the post-season, he relieved solidly in two NLCS games for Los Angeles. Ironically, when the Mets dealt him to the Dodgers, one of the players going the other way was Sid Fernandez—creating a unique situation in which two native-born

Hawai'ians were swapped for each other. Diaz went to James Castle High School, where he starred for the Knights.

Jack DiLauro

Jack DiLauro was part of 1969 World Champ Amazin' Mets, with whom he pitched well (a 2.40 ERA, lower than teammate Nolan Ryan's that year) and earned a World Series ring. But he developed arm trouble, and after spending part of 1970 with the Astros, he went back down to the minors for rehab. Jack spent the last half of 1971 with the Islanders, winning two ballgames.

Dave Dravecky

Major League All-Star Dave Dravecky pitched for the Islanders on his way up to San Diego; in 1982, he went 4-1 for Hawai'i with a 2.48 ERA. He won fourteen for the Padres a year later and in 1984 pitched four and two-thirds scoreless innings in the World Series. He played eight seasons in the majors, finishing with the Giants when a tumor in his pitching arm ended his career prematurely. He's written books about overcoming obstacles and today travels the country making motivational speeches. Dave's uncle Andy Dravecky caught in the Pirates' minor-league system in the 1940s.

Jim Duckworth

Jim Duckworth pitched three seasons on the Isle (1965–67), winning twenty with a sparkling 2.96 ERA. He played four years in the majors (1963–66), working on the mound for the Islanders' parent club (Washington) and finishing up with the A's. The six-foot-four righty overpowered plenty of hitters and struck out a lot of guys—both at "The Show" (220 in 267 innings, with an amazing 74 K's in 64 innings in '65) and in the minors. With Hawai'i, he whiffed more than one batter per frame in each of his three seasons (315 in just 295 innings).

Bob Duliba

Bob Duliba posted a solid single season (1963) in Hawai'i, chalking up eighty-nine K's in ninety-six innings as a bullpen staple and posting a 2.91 ERA in fifty-three contests. His pro career spanned from 1952 through 1971, mostly in the minors, but he did put in seven seasons for the Cardinals, Los Angeles Angels, Red Sox and Kansas City Athletics. He was a pure reliever, ahead of his time—all 176 of Bob's big-league games were from the bullpen. He posted some sensational ERAs: 2.78 as a rookie for St. Louis in 1959 and 2.06 for the Cards in '63 and 1.17 for the Angels the following season. Bob returned to Hawai'i to pitch away games against the Islanders (1966–68) with Vancouver.

Duliba had also played in Hawai'i in 1958, for his military service team, while stationed on the Isles with the marines. Bob was scheduled to rejoin the Islanders' staff in 1972, but back problems forced him to retire. After retiring, though, he threw batting practice for the Oakland A's for a month—a favor from A's owner Charlie Finley, who'd discovered that Duliba was twenty-nine days short of qualifying for his MLB pension. After that, he coached at Wilkes College in Pennsylvania.

Steve Dunning

Stunning Steve Dunning finished his career with the 1978 Islanders, winning six games on the mound. He pitched in the majors for seven seasons and once hit a grand slam off former Islander Diego Segui. Before joining the Islanders' staff, he'd already pitched on the Island during away games when he was with Portland (1972) and Spokane (1974). But Dunning was most stunning in a Pacific Coast League game in 1974, when he was with Spokane. The new Sacramento Solons were playing in makeshift Hughes Stadium, which was not designed for baseball; pop-ups to left cleared the net, and the team hit a record 305 dingers. (After the season, officials confirmed the left-field fence was more like Little League regulation than Triple A regulation.) In the midst of all that, Dunning managed to toss a no-hitter—impressive enough under any circumstance but hard to fathom in those cozy environs.

Elroy "Roy" Face

When he was forty-two years young, three-time all-star Elroy Face tried to squeeze one more year out of his illustrious career and joined the 1970 Islanders. It was his fourth decade pitching professionally. During his sixteen seasons up top (1953–69), the five-foot-eight forkballer led the National League in pitching categories ten times. He had a pretty good season in 1959, going 18-1, and the following year picked up three saves in the Pirates' surprise World Series win over the Yankees. In Honolulu, Face appeared in eight games (even starting one—something he hadn't done since 1957). Always bearing the closer mentality, he fanned nine in ten innings. He didn't play a lot, but his experience helped mold the stellar staff on that championship squad.

Carmen Fanzone

Carmen Fanzone came up with the Red Sox in 1970 and spent the next four seasons with the Cubs, primarily backing up Hall of Famer Ron Santo at third. Over his five-year career, he hit twenty homers in a single season's worth of at-bats. Carmen finished his pro career with Hawai'i in 1975 after previously playing away games there with Tacoma in 1971. Fanzone, a talented trumpet player, played the National Anthem at Wrigley Field several times.

Ed Farmer

Ed Farmer finished his three-decade pitching career in Hawai'i in 1986. "Farmio" went an unsupported 4-7 for the Islanders, with an impressive 2.57 ERA. He'd made the 1980 AL All-Star team for the White Sox, closing fifty-five ballgames and tallying thirty saves. Ed broke in at the major-league level with Cleveland in 1971 and then pitched for seven other big-league clubs, finally hurling for Oakland in 1983. It was a suitcase-laden career marked by volatility. Ed also pitched against the Islanders in 1975 (while with Sacramento), 1978 (Spokane) and 1983–84 (Portland and Tacoma). After playing, he scouted for the Orioles organization for three years. He's been broadcasting ChiSox games on the radio since 1992.

Scott Feldman

At a towering six feet, seven inches, Scott Feldman is the tallest Hawai'i native to play in the majors. Born in Kailua, the righty broke in with the Rangers in 2005 (after Tommy John surgery). He'd progressed rapidly in the minors with some impressive ERAs (2.06, 1.98) before solidifying his spot at "The Show." Over the next eight years with the big club, he gradually moved from the starting rotation to stepping in as a reliever a little more often. But when dealt to the Cubs for 2013, he left the bullpen behind and became a force in the Wrigley Field front five; after a mid-season trade to Baltimore, Scott kept right on starting there. He went 17-8 for the Rangers in 2009 and appeared in five games of the 2011 World Series loss against St. Louis.

Sid Fernandez

In 1986, Sid Fernandez was the first Hawai'i native to become an MLB All-Star (he finished 16-6 that year), and he repeated as a National League All-Star the following year. He played on the state champ Little League team in Honolulu and led his Kaiser High School Cougars to the state title after pitching a no-hitter in his first start. He's the only Kaiser alum to make the majors so far, but three others (Brant McCreadie and Mark Stillwell before him and Colby Ho afterward) also signed pro contracts.

Fernandez wore the number fifty on his major-league jerseys to celebrate his roots with all five teams for which he suited up: the Dodgers, Mets, Orioles, Phillies and Astros. "El Sid" pitched fifteen seasons in the majors (1983–97) and contributed to the Mets' 1988 World Championship, pitching lights-out ball in the Fall Classic (whiffing ten batters in six and two-thirds innings on a 1.35 ERA). He led the National League in win-loss percentage (.737, 14-5) the following season. Later, he coached the amateur Hawai'i Island Movers, helped the mayor of Honolulu boost youth sports, participated in celebrity golf tourneys to raise funds for kids' sports programs and worked at his own foundation to benefit young people. He's a member of the Hawai'i Sports Hall of Fame and is one of seven baseball players on the *Sports Illustrated*/CNN 1999 list of "The 50 Greatest Hawai'i Sports Figures," coming in at number ten.

Mike Fetters

Half-Samoan Mike Fetters is one of half a dozen Iolani School grads who signed pro contracts, and along with fellow Raider alum Kila Ka'aihue, he is one of two who made it to the bigs. Fetters manned the mound in the majors for sixteen seasons (1989–2004), appearing on the rosters of eight ball clubs. He finished in his loop's top-ten saves leaders three times, rounding out his career with an even one hundred. He'd previously pitched for Team USA in the 1985 Intercontinental Cup, and since then Fetters has worked in the Arizona Diamondbacks office and is one of the club's radio color men. He also acts as a sports agent out of Beverly Hills.

Brian Fisher

Moundsman Brian Fisher was a true journeyman. Born in Honolulu, he pitched his high school ball in Colorado, got drafted by the Braves, debuted for the 1985 Yankees (two seasons), moved on to Pittsburgh (three years), put in a single season for the Astros and finally wrapped up with one year in Seattle. Brian's best big-league season was 1987, when he won eleven games for the Bucs. In his rookie year, he was selected to the Topps All-Star Rookie Team, racked up fourteen saves and a 2.38 ERA (tenth best in the American League) and placed sixth in Rookie of the Year balloting.

Al Fitzmorris

Al Fitzmorris pitched in the American League for ten years, from 1969 to 1978. He won sixteen games for the 1975 Royals and fifteen the following year. He also played for the Indians and Angels. He finished with Hawai'i in 1979, winning a couple ballgames in limited action. Al didn't get a lot of press because he was in a small market during the prime of his career, but he posted ERAs of 2.83, 2.79 and 3.06—which would've won twenty games and put him on all-star rosters if he'd been in a bigger pond.

Gene Freese

Gene Freese logged a dozen solid seasons in "The Show," breaking in with the 1955 Pirates. He played for five other teams through 1966. Gene smacked fourteen homers as a rookie and twenty-three for the '59 Phils.

In '61, he hit twenty-six homers, helping the Reds to the World Series. Primarily a third baseman, Freese also played a variety of other positions in both the infield and outfield. He was a star for the Islanders in 1967, hitting twenty-eight doubles and fifteen homers to go along with a .274 average. His brother George also played three years in the majors, and Gene managed two seasons in the Texas League.

Dave Freisleben

Dave Freisleben pitched four seasons in Hawai'i (1973–74 and 1976–77). He was the staff star in '73, going 16-8 on a 2.82 ERA and whiffing 206 in 195 innings. He also pitched six seasons with the Padres, Indians and Blue Jays during the '70s.

Jim French

Catcher Jim French spent parts of three campaigns (1965–67) in Hawai'i, shuttling up and down between the Islanders and the parent Senators. He spent seven seasons in the AL, backing up All-Star Paul Casanova; he broke in during 1965, batting a solid .297 in limited play. A classic catcher, he was stocky (five feet, seven inches), had an arm like a cannon and was a smart handler of pitchers. Mr. French graduated from Ohio University and earned a master's degree in finance from Indiana University and his law degree from John Marshall Law School.

ADRIAN GARRETT INF

Adrian Garrett

Before playing his last three seasons for Hiroshima, Adrian Garrett finished his U.S. career as a Hawai'i Islander in 1976. And "Smokey" finished strong, too, hitting .310 with nine homers in just 126 at-bats. He's a double Hall of Famer, honored in both the Tacoma Baseball Hall (for his Pacific Coast League exploits) and the Appleton Hall (for managing the 1982 Foxes to the Midwest League pennant). Adrian smacked nearly 400 home runs (393 over nineteen seasons): 280 in the minors, 102 in Japan and 11 at "The

Show" (1961–79). He led his league in dingers several times (43 for Tacoma in 1971—plenty of those against the Islanders).

Yet despite all this experience and all these heroics, Mr. Garrett never seemed to get the chance he deserved in the majors; the Braves, Cubs, A's and Angels all called him up for a few games over the course of eight seasons and then sent him back down to Triple A to terrorize the pitchers there. He finally looked like he was getting a shot with California in 1975 (he hit six homers in 107 at-bats, on pace for more than thirty for the season) but ended up in Wichita (where he hit .321—with power, of course). Smokey's brother Wayne was with the Mets for years, including the '69 world championship team. Adrian has been the hitting coach for the Louisville Bats (the Reds' Triple-A farm team) for nearly a decade.

Rod Gaspar

Outfielder Rod Gaspar played for the Islanders for six straight seasons (1971–76), batting .300 in '73. He's best known as being a part of the 1969 Amazin' Mets, and he's got a World Series ring to show for it. (In fact, he scored the winning run in Game 5.) He played for the Mets in 1970 as well and with the Padres in 1971 and 1974. Rod's son Cade played minor-league ball for three years.

Eli Grba

Eli Grba needed to buy a vowel, but he was a regular part of the Islanders' starting rotation in 1963 and 1965. Before and between those years, he played for the Yankees (1959–60) and expansion Los Angeles Angels (1961–63). He didn't pitch in the '60 World Series, but Manager Casey Stengel let him pinch run in Game 6. He helped the hapless Angels with eleven tough wins in their first year. After retiring, he managed in the minors for three seasons.

Doug Griffin

Second-baseman Doug Griffin led the Islanders' championship charge in 1970, earning his ride to "The Show." Doug hit .326 and paced the PCL with thirty-five steals en route to eight years in the American League (including a 1975 World Series appearance with the Red Sox). While stationed at Pearl Harbor with the U.S. Navy (1967–68), Doug's military all-star team had finished second at the National Baseball Congress World Series.

Tony Gwynn

Tony Gwynn, one of the game's all-time great hitters, beat up on Pacific Coast League pitchers while in Hawai'i. During the 1982 season, Tony delighted Islander fans by batting a torrid .328 with power and speed and hardly a strikeout to be found. The bad news for locals, of course, was that he was hitting so well that the parent Padres called him up mid-season. Gwynn's Hall of Fame career needs little introduction. In twenty years (all with the Padres), from 1982 to 2001, he hit .338 (.394 in '94), smacked 3,141 hits, stole 319 bases, made fifteen All-Star team—the litany is endless. And of course, he was the batting star in Honolulu when his Padres played the first-ever major-league games there in 1997; he smacked four hits, the only player to get hits in all three games.

Jimmie Hall

Two-time MLB All-Star Jimmie Hall played eight seasons up top, from 1963 to 1970. He started strong with the Twins, swatting thirty-three homers as a rookie and then twenty-five and twenty in his two Midsummer Classic seasons. In '65, he played in the World Series against the Dodgers. Jimmie also patrolled the outfield for the five other clubs. He finished his career with Hawai'i by batting .280 in twenty-one games in 1971.

Larry Haney

Larry Haney played in the majors for twelve seasons (1966–78), winning a World Series ring with the 1974 Oakland A's. In the middle of that stretch, he caught for the 1972 Islanders. The following season, he came back with Tucson to play a few more away games in Honolulu. Larry's big-league history includes stops with Baltimore, the brand-new Seattle Pilots, the Athletics, the Cards and, finally, the Brewers. He started with a bang, smacking a homer in his first game. He's also achieved cult-like status among classic-era baseball card collectors because Topps used the same photo from his 1968 card on his 1969 card but reversed the negative…so Larry appears as a left-handed catcher. After playing, he coached for the Brewers (1978–91) before heading upstairs and working for the team over the course of another two decades. His son Chris pitched in the majors for eleven seasons and in Japan for one.

Jim Hannan

Jim Hannan started as a reliever and evolved into a starter. He spent ten seasons at "The Show," mostly with the Senators, from 1962 to 1971 (he also suited up with the Tigers and Brewers during his final season). Jim's best year was 1968, when he had a 10-6 mark and a nifty 3.01 ERA. He was an ace of the '65 Hawai'i staff, going 12-7 (before picking up a win for the Senators, too). Jim spent all of 1966 with Washington and then split '67 between the two levels. He's a Notre Dame grad, just like Hall of Famers Carl Yastrzemski and Cap Anson.

Chuck Hartenstein

Chuck Hartenstein played and coached for the Islanders and also pitched against Hawai'i for several seasons (1967–76) with Tacoma, Tucson and Phoenix. He went 17-7 in his two Islander campaigns, tying for the team lead with eleven wins in '76. In the majors, he played for five clubs over six seasons (1965–77). Chuck then coached for Cleveland in 1979 before coming back to Honolulu to be the Islanders pitching coach from 1980 to 1986. His staffs were so successful that he caught the attention of the Brewers, who called him up to coach in Milwaukee. He got his nickname, "Twiggy," from the famous '60s model.

Ron Hassey

Ron Hassey played a few games for the final-season Islanders in 1987 after catching road games in Honolulu with Portland ('78) and Tacoma ('79). He'd caught for half a dozen big-league teams over fourteen seasons (1978–91), the first seven of those with Cleveland. He's the only backstop in the history of the game to catch two different perfect games—ten years apart (Len Barker with the 1981 Indians and Dennis Martinez with the 1991 Expos). He played in two World Series with the A's (1988 and 1990); ironically, Ron got a ring with the A's in '89, although he didn't play that year. (He had the best view in the house for Kirk Gibson's miracle homer in '88—Ron was catching Eck that night.) Hassey later managed in the minors, scouted for the Yankees, coached for the Rockies and Cards and served upstairs in the Diamondbacks' office. His dad, Bill, and his son Brad played in the minors.

Ed Herrmann

Ed Herrmann caught for eleven seasons in the majors (1967–78), mostly with the White Sox and then briefly with four other clubs. He was named to the 1974 American League All-Star team on the basis of his superb pitcher-handling skills. His best year in front of the plate (1970) yielded a .283 average and nineteen home runs. Ed spent the middle of 1968 with the Islanders, swatting five homers in just 139 at-bats. His grandfather Marty "Lefty" Herrmann pitched a single hitless inning for the 1918 Brooklyn Robins (before they became the Trolley Dodgers). Since retiring, Ed has scouted for the Royals.

Jack Hiatt

Jack Hiatt played for Hawai'i twice—once on the way up and once on the way down. His first stop was at the end of the 1963 season, following which he started 1964 by socking twenty-three homers and hitting .308. In '73, he hit a solid .290 with ten round-trippers. (He also played against the Islanders with Tacoma in '65 and Phoenix in '66.) In between his Honolulu assignments, Jack caught in the majors for eight seasons for five teams. After retiring, he coached for the Cubbies and managed in the minors from 1975 to 1988, winning more than five hundred ballgames. In 1991, he became the Giants' director of player development—a position he held for sixteen years. He still serves in the Giants system as a scouting consultant.

Roy Hobbs

Roy Hobbs was a natural, and he performed stellar feats as both pitcher and power hitter. Between his 1923 tryout with the Chicago Cubs and his 1939 reemergence in New York, his career is sketchy…but legend holds that he crossed paths with Babe Ruth and may have barnstormed over to Hawaiʻi and played for one of the *Haole* teams in the Plantation League.

Charlie Hough

Charlie Hough holds the Hawaiʻi-born ballplayer records for longest big-league career (twenty-five years), career wins (216) and wins in a season (18 with the '87 Rangers—at age thirty-nine). The All-Star (1986) knuckleballer appeared in three World Series for the Dodgers (alas, all losses) and converted from reliever to starter. Hough broke in with Los Angeles in 1970 and stayed there for more than a decade (including going 12-8 with a 2.21 ERA in 1976) before going to the Rangers in mid-1980. He stayed in Texas for more than a decade and then spent two years with the White Sox before finally finishing up with the Marlins in 1993–94, retiring at forty-six. He's a member of the Rangers' Hall of Fame.

Hough, who was born in Tripler Army Med Center in 1948, pitched in his native Hawaiʻi for three seasons, playing in away games against the Islanders for Spokane (1970–71) and Albuquerque (1972). For both teams, his manager was Tommy Lasorda, who would later be his skipper with the Dodgers. After retiring, Hough served as pitching coach for the Dodgers for a few years and also in the minors for a bunch of teams. He's currently listed as a senior advisor for player development on the Dodgers' chart. His dad, Dick, had played third base in the New York Giants' organization back in 1933.

Mike Huff

Mike Huff got off to a good start, smacking a base hit in his first big-league at-bat. Better still, he did it against future Hall of Famer Tom Glavine. Huff broke in with the Dodgers in 1989 and stayed at "The Show" for seven seasons, also patrolling the outfield for the Indians, White Sox and Jays. His Chicago squad made the post-season in 1993, and the following year with Toronto, he recorded a .304 batting average as the Jays' fourth man in the outfield. In ten minor-league seasons—most of them in Triple-A—he hit .307. Huff holds an interesting stat: each of his nine career major-league home runs was a solo shot. These days, Huff is serving as a valuable utilityman in the booth, backing up the regular ChiSox TV team.

Steve Huntz

Steve Huntz had one of the longest playing careers as an Islander (four seasons, 1974–77) and was the consummate utility man, playing first, second, short and a little outfield. He also caught a game, and for all we know, he might have snuck up into the stands to sell some shave ice, too. During six other seasons, he played away games in Honolulu while with four other PCL teams, making him a ten-year regular at Honolulu Stadium. During his fourteen-year career in the minors, he smacked precisely one hundred homers. He played in parts of five seasons (1967–75) in the big leagues for the Cardinals, White Sox and Padres and once hit two homers in a game off former World Series MVP Mickey Lolich.

Jabbo Jablonski

Jabbo Jablonski was a major-league veteran and a World War II veteran (one of the last remaining active players) when he joined the first-season Islanders in 1961. He spent eight seasons in the majors, mostly manning third for the Cardinals, Redlegs, Giants and Kansas City Athletics before playing to sea. As a rookie in 1953, he hit twenty-one homers, and he was named to the National League All-Star team the following year.

Jabbo hit 14 homers in his half season in Honolulu, where he also taught the younger guys a thing or two about the game. From there, Jabbo spent several more seasons in the minors, finally retiring after the 1964 season at the age of thirty-seven. In 1963, he returned to Hawai'i for some away contests with Dallas. During his minor-league career (six seasons on the way up and six on the way back down), Jabbo clubbed 215 homers and 240 two-baggers and had a lifetime average just a shade under .300 (he finished at .297, hitting .326 as a rookie and .341 with Dallas when he was thirty-four).

Sonny Jackson

Shortstop Sonny Jackson played twelve years at the major-league level (1963–74) with the Houston Colt .45s/Astros and Atlanta Braves. As a rookie, he led the National League in singles (160) and sacrifice hits (27), compiling a .292 average en route to finishing third in Rookie of the Year balloting. He tore up Islanders pitching in 1965, visiting Honolulu for PCL games with Oklahoma City, and then suited up for the Hawai'i ballclub ten seasons later. After retiring, Sonny coached and managed in the minors and coached in the majors for the Braves, Giants and Cubs.

Jerry Johnson

Jerry Johnson pitched ten years in the majors. His stellar 1971 performance for the Giants (12-9, 2.97 ERA, eighteen saves) earned him Cy Young/MVP votes. He broke in with Philadelphia in 1968 and then played for six other big-league clubs until 1977. Jerry was a 1975 Pacific Coast League All-Star for the Hawai'i Islanders, finishing with a sparkling 10-3 mark and a 2.94 ERA. He was back with the Islanders the following year, winning seven and pitching well enough to earn a final trip back to the majors. Before that, he'd been with the San Diego Padres in 1968—their last year as a PCL team—so he played road games in Honolulu Stadium, too.

Kila Ka'aihue

With his great islander name, Kila Ka'aihue was born in Kailua and played high school ball for the fabled Iolani School Raiders. This kid has owned the minors, and he still has some solid big-league hopes. He debuted in 2008 for the Royals, with whom he played three seasons before heading over to Oakland. After a year with the A's, he was dealt to the Diamondbacks, who assigned him to their Triple A club in Reno (where he hit .313, with power, in 2013). Kila's younger brother, Kala, toiled in the minors for eight seasons (starting in 2005) but never got his ticket punched to "The Show."

Fred Kendall

Fred Kendall caught for the Padres from 1969 to 1980, interrupted by one-season stops in Cleveland and Boston. A superb handler of pitchers, he was voted Most Valuable Padre by his teammates in '73. His brief 1971 stay in Hawai'i was his ticket out of the minors; he hit .324 with plenty of power in just eleven games, having been equally effective for the competition (Salt Lake) in Honolulu in 1970. Kendall later managed in the minors and served as a bullpen coach for the Royals. His son Jason caught in the majors for fifteen years.

Willie Kirkland

Willie Kirkland hit more than 100 homers in the majors, more than 100 in the minors and more than 100 in Japan. He smacked 34 of those for the 1967 Islanders—a single-season team record that still stands. Willie roamed outfields for nine years at "The Show," starting as a charter San Francisco Giant in 1958 and then playing for Cleveland, Baltimore and Washington until 1966. His best seasons were 1960, when he hit 21 homers for the Giants, and 1961, when he hit 27 home runs and ninety-five RBIs for Cleveland (he also smacked three dingers in one game that year). After that, he spent one year in Honolulu and then kept going west until he ended up in the Far East. Willie finally retired after six more seasons of busting fences for Hanshin, at the age of thirty-nine. In all, he belted 176 home runs in just six minor-league seasons and had a career batting mark of .302.

Ed Kirkpatrick

Long-lasting Ed Kirkpatrick was a major-leaguer for seventeen years, from 1962 to 1977. He caught, played outfield and manned a few other posts for five teams but never got to the World Series. "Spanky" did great in Hawai'i in 1963, hitting .352 with power, but his numbers were off the next season. He also played plenty of away games in Honolulu while with Seattle (1965 and '67) and Salt Lake ('78) before playing in Mexico.

Ron Kline

Righty Ron Kline pitched for nine big-league clubs from 1952 to 1970. A workhorse starter/reliever, he was often near the top of his league in categories such as saves, games finished, batters faced, innings pitched, shutouts and, because of usually being on second-division teams, losses (he never got to a World Series). After an eighteen-year absence, the wise and experienced sage returned to the minors in 1970 to help the Islanders during their championship run. Mr. Kline went 4-0 for Hawai'i. After retiring, he was elected mayor of his hometown, Callery, Pennsylvania.

Bobby Knoop

Bobby Knoop made the American League All-Star team in 1966, when he led the league with eleven triples for the California Angels. He played in the majors for nine years for the Angels, the White Sox and the Royals. Best known as a slick-fielding second-baseman, Bobby won three straight Gold Gloves (1966–68). He was such an acrobatic fielder that he earned the nickname "Nureyev."

Bobby starred for the Islanders in 1962 and 1963, pounding twenty home runs his second year. He'd also played against the inaugural-year Islanders in 1961 with San Diego and Vancouver. After retiring, Knoop coached and managed in the minors for a few seasons. He returned to the bigs in 1975 to start four decades of major-league coaching with the Angels, ChiSox and Toronto. He tried to retire in 2000 and started helping out at a high school near his home in Arizona, but the Rockies came calling for his scouting and player development prowess, so he obliged from 2008 to 2009. He went back to high school but once again came back to coach with the Angels in 2013—making him one of an elite few who suited up for the Angels in all four of their geographical gestations. Along the way, he pinch-managed the Halos to a 1-1 record in 1994.

Shane Komine

Honolulu-born Shane Kenji Komine has a pretty cool nickname: the Hawai'ian Punch-Out. After playing for the Kalani High Falcons (where Ryan Kurosaki and Lenn Sakata played earlier), Shane set the University of Nebraska school record for career wins. Signed by the A's, he played for the big club in 2006–07. He had all the potential in the world, but arm problems led to Tommy John surgery. Shane is considered the third Japanese American major-leaguer, after Travis Ishikawa and Sakata (a questionable stat since Japanese-born players like Ichiro don't count in that category). He pitched eight seasons in the minors (2002–09), going 11-8 for the 2006 Sacramento River Cats.

Fred Kuhaulua

Honolulu-born Fred Kuhaulua holds a pretty nifty career mark in the majors: a perfect 1-0 record on the mound. He pitched for the Angels (1977) and Padres (1981); in between, he was with Chunichi in Japan. In all, Fred put in a decade in the pros (1972–82), starting when he was just nineteen. He finished up as a four-year Islanders ace, winning ten games a year from 1979 to 1981. Before that, in 1977, he tried out Honolulu Stadium during away games with Salt Lake. Another claim to fame for Fred is that his lone major-league base hit came off knuckleballing Hall of Famer Phil Niekro. Athletic prowess runs in Fred's family; his uncle Levi Stanley played for the Hawai'ians in the World Football League in the '70s.

Clarence Kumalae

In these days of Googling whatever you want, anybody who played in the Major Leagues comes up quickly and on multiple pages. Not so for Clarence Kumalae—although in reality, this native Hawai'ian was a big part of pro ball (and, in fact, the Major Leagues) throughout the 1930s and '40s. To understand, you need to know the Wrigley connection.

Chewing-gum magnate William Wrigley owned the Chicago Cubs and, of course, Wrigley Field. He also owned the Los Angeles Angels, then a minor-league club in the Pacific Coast League, and their stadium, which was also called Wrigley Field. He also owned Catalina Island, off the coast of Southern California, where the Cubs held spring training from 1921 to 1951. Avalon, the main town on Catalina, had a semipro team called the Catalina Cubs, whose grandstand (it was a bit too small to be considered a ballpark) was also called Wrigley Field. These Cubs played against other regional teams fielded by oil companies and motion picture studios like Paramount Pictures.

Kumalae earned a tryout with the Angels in 1933 (the same year Tony Robello made the majors and a year before Prince Oana), played for the semipro squad and went back to Chicago to work as a batting-practice pitcher at the main Wrigley Field. He did this for years, suiting up in a Cubs' uniform in the locker room with All-Stars and Hall of Famers alike. In those days, the Cubs made it to the World Series on a regular basis, so this Hawai'i native pitched batting practice before World Series games in 1935 and 1938. They kept him around because he knew how to serve it up to warm up the Cubbie bats. "He was a left-hander, and he could throw strikes like nobody," recalled Hub Kittle, who won a World Series ring as a pitching coach for the 1982 Cards. "He'd hit a cup if you put it up there…knock it right off." Along the way, Kumalae also "officially" played a few seasons in the minors (Omaha, Cedar Rapids and Vancouver).

So no, Hawai'i's own Clarence Kumalae doesn't show up in the record books, but the players back then considered him just as much one of the guys as his more well-known contemporaries.

Ryan Kurosaki

Honolulu-born Ryan Yoshitomo Kurosaki is often listed as the first Japanese American to play in the Major Leagues, but he was actually the second, as fellow Hawai'ian Mike Lum beat him to the punch by eight seasons. Ryan played for the Kalani High School Falcons and then pitched at the University of Nebraska before signing with the Cardinals in 1974. He quickly made his way to St. Louis and pitched seven games in 1975 before heading back to the minors and ultimately completing an eight-year pro career in 1980.

Craig Kusick

Craig Kusick was a big deal in the Pacific Coast League for quite a few years. As a Tacoma Twin, he battered the Islanders in 1973 (.305, twenty-seven homers) and 1974 (.328), and he was doing enough damage in '75 that the parent club called him up. In 1980, Craig returned to the PCL—this time with Hawai'i, thankfully—where he hit .305 with seventeen homers in a partial season. Back in Hawai'i in '81, Kusick hit .277 with punch. In the midst of this, he played seven seasons with the Twins and Jays, hitting a few homers there as well. His son Craig Jr. played college football in Wisconsin and went on to be a pro quarterback in the Arena Football League.

Dave LaRoche

Dave LaRoche turned in one of the Islanders' all-time great pitching seasons in 1970, leading the championship drive by going a perfect 6-0 with a microscopic 1.24 ERA and sixty-seven strikeouts in just fifty-eight innings. During his fourteen years in the bigs (1970–83), Dave pitched for five teams. As a Cleveland Indian, he made American League All-Star squads in 1976 and 1977. Since retiring, he's coached in the minors and majors (White Sox and Mets) since 1984. He's currently with the Las Vegas 51s in the Blue Jays' system. His sons, Adam and Andy, are currently playing in the majors.

Johnnie LeMaster

Johnnie LeMaster spent a lot of time in Honolulu. He played against Hawai'i on the way up to his twelve-year major-league career, and he was one of the final Islanders in 1987. Johnnie played three seasons (1975–77) with Phoenix before becoming the regular shortstop in San Francisco. There, he played eleven seasons for the Giants and then had stops in Cleveland and Pittsburgh. LeMaster spent 1986 in the Expos farm system and started 1987 with Tacoma in the PCL but finished the year with the home team on O'ahu.

Johnnie hit an inside-the-park homer in his first major-league at-bat—the only player in the storied history of the game to accomplish that feat. Ironically, ten years later, he also legged out an inside-the-park dinger for his final big-league home run. He also played Islandball in the Puerto Rican Winter League. After his pro career, he served as the head baseball coach at Pikeville University in Kentucky, where he became the winningest coach in the school's history and in 2007 was elected to its hall of fame. The university's diamond has been named LeMaster Field in his honor.

Don Leppert

All-Star Don Leppert played only one season for the Islanders—1965—but he made quite an impression. The big backstop hit .338 with power, and as a seasoned big-league veteran, he handled the young pitchers effectively. Lep, who'd played for the Pirates (1961–62) and the Senators

(1963–64), got started with a bang, smacking a homer in his first big-league at-bat. After he retired, he spent eighteen years coaching in the majors with Pittsburgh, Toronto and Houston. Don is a member of the Indiana Baseball Hall of Fame.

Frank Linzy

During his eleven-year major-league career (1963–74), Frank Linzy pitched for the Giants, Cards, Brewers and Phillies. As a rookie, he finished third in National League Rookie of the Year voting with a 1.43 ERA and forty saves. Although a reliever, he won fourteen games for the '69 Giants. Frank finished up with the 1975 Islanders, shutting down late-inning rallies with a 3.05 ERA.

Winston Llenas

Winston Llenas is one of the Islanders' all-time greats. He played briefly for Hawai'i in 1963 and '64, but his fireworks started when he returned in the summer of '69, when he hit .361 and belted twenty-three doubles and twelve homers despite playing only half a season. The following year, he spearheaded the championship drive with twenty home runs, a league-leading 108 RBIs and a .339 average. Unfortunately for the locals, he was across the Coast League with Salt Lake City in '71, pounding vengeance against the Islanders. Llenas put in twelve seasons in the minors to go along with six with the California Angels, eight in the Mexican Leagues and another in Japan—a twenty-three-year career that lasted from 1961 to 1983.

Although Winston's major-league career, four seasons with the Angels between 1968 and 1975, was relatively uneventful, he did lead the league in pinch hits in 1973. He also managed in Mexico and in the Angels' organization before going on to coach for Toronto, and he currently owns a team in his native Dominican Republic—where he's won numerous championship titles as player, manager, general manager and team president. His brother Gus played a few years in the Phillies organization.

Mike Lum

Honolulu's Michael Ken-Wai Lum was a baseball and football star (the quarterback was actually awarded a scholarship to BYU) for the Theodore Roosevelt High School Rough Riders before starting his fifteen-year major-league career (1967–81) with the Braves, Reds and Cubs. In 1967, Mike became the second Japanese player (after Masanori Murakami) and the first Japanese American to make it to "The Show." (Filipino Bobby Balcena, a Hawai'i Islander alum, was the first Asian to reach the big leagues.)

Mr. Lum is the only player who ever pinch-hit for Hank Aaron, and he has a World Series ring from Cincy's 1976 triumph. For years, he held the record for most major-league home runs hit by a Hawai'i-born ballplayer (ninety), but Shane Victorino passed him in 2013. He coached in Japan and in the U.S. Minor Outlying Islands, and when the Hawai'i Winter Baseball League got started, he came back home to lead the North Shore Honu ("Sea Turtles") to a league championship. When the league folded, he came back to the mainland, where he currently coaches in the Pirates' farm system. Mike is one of seven baseball players on the *Sports Illustrated*/CNN 1999 list of "The 50 Greatest Hawai'i Sports Figures," coming in at the thirteenth spot.

Keith Luuloa

Keith Luuloa had a brief big-league career (six games for the Angels in 2000) but played well, earning a lifetime batting average of .333. Keith was born in Honolulu on O'ahu but lived in a tiny village called Kaunakakai on Moloka'i and played for the Moloka'i High Farmers in Ho'olehua. His team took ferryboats to its "road" games because the scholastic budget didn't allow for inter-island flights. In all, Keith played a number of positions for a number of clubs during his eleven-year professional career. He was the first big-leaguer from Moloka'i.

Steve Lyons

Steve Lyons played nine uneventful years in the big leagues (except the time he dropped his pants in the infield, thus earning his nickname). "Psycho" also spent a rather uneventful year with the final (1987) Islanders, hitting .287 in forty-seven games. His 1985–93 career at "The Show" included stops with the Red Sox, White Sox, Braves and Expos. The consummate utility man, he eventually played all nine positions in the majors (yep, he even caught four games and pitched twice) but mostly roamed the outfield and manned the hot corner.

Lyons's minor-league career was quite sane in comparison. Over eight seasons (1981–93), he hit for pretty good power and showed plenty of hustle, stealing forty-seven bases one year and thirty-five two other times. He also pitched half a dozen times over three seasons.

Steve went on to broadcasting, including several years calling games for the FOX network, and currently works for the Dodgers doing a post-game show and calling road games (since Vin Scully trimmed his travel schedule). Steve is also one of the few big-leaguers to pen an autobiography. His is titled *Steve Lyons: PSYCHOanalysis*.

Jerry Manuel

Jerry Manuel managed the New York Mets for a few seasons—a hallowed baseball job first held by Casey Stengel, then Gil Hodges (who led the 1969 Amazin' Mets to a world championship) and, later, Joe Torre. Manuel previously skippered the 2000 White Sox to a division win and was named American League Manager of the Year. He played parts of five seasons in the majors with Detroit, San Diego and Montreal and worked thirteen seasons in the minors (including several as player-coach and player-manager).

Jerry was a backup shortstop on the 1982 Islanders team with Tony Gwynn, and he hit within 132 points of Tony's average. Jerry came out of the Cordova High School Lancers program in Rancho Cordova, California (near Sacramento), which has produced nearly a dozen major-leaguers and twenty-six pro ballplayers (including no-hit pitcher Chris Bosio, Geoff Jenkins, Max Venable and Randy Lerch). While there, the multi-sport star also received football college scholarship offers from Ohio State and USC, among others. Years later, his son Anthony played five seasons in the minors, and his daughter, Angela, reached the semifinals (one hundred meters) in the 2000 U.S. Olympic Track and Field Trials. His nephew Marcellous Manuel also played three seasons in the minor leagues. These days, Jerry is an analyst for the MLB Network.

Onan Masaoka

The first major-leaguer from the Big Island of Hawai'i was pitcher Onan Kainoa Satoshi Masaoka. Born in Hilo, Onan started out at Hilo High and was transferred to Waiakea High when it opened in 1976 (to the chagrin of his Hilo High baseball coach, no doubt). The Dodgers drafted him in 1995, and Onan debuted for the blue club in 1999. He pitched part of two seasons, striking out eighty-eight guys in ninety-three and two-third innings from the bullpen, winning three and saving one. Like a few of his other Hawai'ian mates, he did get to wear number fifty at "The Show" in honor of his state's statehood. He struck out pretty much everybody he faced in the minors—starting off with seventy-five whiffs in a mere forty-nine innings at Yakima at the tender age of seventeen! After a few more seasons in the minors, he returned to Hawai'i to go to UH before making a few minor-league tryouts several years later.

John Matias

John Matias was the first native-born Hawai'ian from Farrington High School to make the Major Leagues, but he was not the first overall; a mere sixty-one years earlier, Bill Yohe (born on the mainland) also got to the top. (Wally Yonamine attended in between and made the Japanese Baseball Hall of Fame—not to mention playing in the NFL—but didn't reach the big leagues.) Matias belted four homers (and knocked in all nine of the Governors' runs) to win the 1962 state championship, played in Honolulu Stadium. After that, his local team played in the American Legion World Series on the mainland. His younger brother, Bob, also played two years of minor-league ball for the same teams in the Baltimore farm system, and later, his son John Jr. starred at the University of Hawai'i.

Matias played for the White Sox in 1970, swatting two home runs in his brief stint. All together, he put in eighteen seasons as a pro, starting in 1963 and wrapping up with his own Hawai'i Islanders in 1980 (he'd also played for the Honolulu club in 1972 and 1973, smacking twenty homers in '72.) Having signed with the Orioles right out of high school, he got off to a hot start, hitting .433 (with power) in the Appalachian League at just eighteen. After a few years in the White Sox, Twins and Padres' organizations, John jumped to the Mexican League, where he hit .305 and also won twenty-six games as a pitcher. After six years south of the border, he came back to Hawai'i to wrap up his career with the Islanders in 1980. Matias is Joe DeSa's uncle.

Lee Maye

Outfielder Lee Maye slugged his way through the majors for thirteen campaigns (1959–71) with five teams. He led the National League with forty-four doubles in 1964 (for the Milwaukee Brewers) while hitting .304, and he batted .300 or better in two other partial seasons. Lee spent nine seasons in the minors too, hitting .311 (with power) for the 1971 Islanders and .285 (with power) for Hawai'i the following year. His lifetime minor-league average is .309, which includes three years above .330 and 128 homers. Mr. Maye was also an accomplished R&B singer, performing at venues like the Hollywood Bowl. Maye was often confused with Lee May, who played at the same time. (In 1965, Mr. May tore up Hawai'i pitching with the PCL San Diego Padres, hitting .321 and blasting thirty-four homers).

Mike McCormick

He's somewhat overlooked today, but in 1967, Mike McCormick won the National League Cy Young Award (the year after Sandy Koufax and before Bob Gibson) in a league that also included guys like Tom Seaver, Steve Carlton, Fergie Jenkins and teammates Gaylord Perry and Juan Marichal. Mike pitched for the Islanders at the end of his stellar major-league career, splitting 1972 between Phoenix and Hawai'i and the following season between Hawai'i and Tacoma. All together, Mike won twenty-two Pacific Coast League games during those two seasons.

McCormick played his first major-league game at the age of seventeen, breaking in at the Polo Grounds for the Giants. Along with Willie Mays, Mike was the last remaining New York Giant on the San Francisco roster in the '70s. A four-time All-Star, Mike led the league in wins (twenty-two) in 1967, paced the circuit with a 2.70 ERA in 1960 and was frequently near the top of the heap in strikeouts, shutouts and complete games. He also pitched for the Orioles and Senators before returning to the Giants and then putting in his final two seasons with the Yankees and Royals. Years after retiring, he still runs fantasy baseball camps for his Giants.

Jim McManus

First baseman Jim McManus was a star of the Hawai'i Islanders' inaugural 1961 season, smacking twenty-one homers and hitting .275. During his brief (five games) stay with the Kansas City Athletics the year before, he hit .308 with power. But the guys at the majors didn't see what they were looking for in Jim, so he went to Japan and played two seasons for the Taiyo Whales.

Bill Melton

All-Star Bill Melton, the 1971 American League home run champ, played ten years in the majors—eight with the White Sox, one with the Angels and another with Cleveland. The third baseman smacked ten dingers in a partial season for Hawai'i in 1968. Since retiring, "Beltin' Bill" has been broadcasting games for his old SouthSiders.

Joey Meyer

Honolulu's own Joey Meyer may have been the first major-leaguer to tip the scales at three hundred pounds. He played both baseball and football for the University of Hawai'i Rainbow Warriors before terrorizing minor-league pitching. As a rookie, he hit .320 with thirty homers and 102 RBIs and was named the 1984 Midwest League Player of the Year. The following year, he hit thirty-seven home runs (good enough for the Texas League title), knocked in 137 runs and batted .304. Next was a twenty-four-dinger campaign for Vancouver in the Pacific Coast League (which, of course, included a triumphant return to Honolulu to play away games against the Islanders) and a 582-foot altitude-aided homer for the Denver Zephyrs before Milwaukee finally got around to calling him up (he'd already swatted twenty-nine round-trippers in just half a season).

Joey immediately became the Brewers' starting first baseman in 1988, but numerous injuries took their toll. He hit eleven homers and eighteen doubles (on a respectable .263 clip) in a partial rookie season, but his pace fell in 1989. He finished the year in Denver with solid but not-as-stellar numbers, played for Yokohama in 1990 (26 homers) and then tried again in the minors, putting in a so-so half season with Buffalo in 1991 before hanging up his massive cleats to retire back to his native Hawai'i. In all, Joey smacked 135 home runs in the minors and 18 at "The Show." He holds the distinction of being the only player to hit a walk-off game winner against Roger Clemens.

Joe Moeller

Joe Moeller was part of those great Dodger pitching staffs, relieving for Sandy Koufax and Don Drysdale, among others—and he was a Hawai'i Islander, too. Joe pitched for Los Angeles from 1962 (when he was just nineteen) to 1971, appearing in the 1966 World Series. He first played in Honolulu a few weeks after graduating from high school, for visiting Spokane in PCL contests. Joe came back a few times during four other seasons with Spokane in the '60s and with the 1973 Eugene Ems. He was with Hawai'i for a few weeks in '73 after having spent all of 1972 there; that year, he struck out 119 in 160 innings and won eight ballgames. He's scouted for the Marlins for more than a decade, and although he didn't get a World Series ring with the Dodgers, he got one with the Miami club in 2003.

Sid Monge

Sid Monge was a perfect 1-0 for the 1985 Islanders, closing fourteen games. He'd just won a World Series ring with Detroit (in '84) to complete his ten-season big-league career. A 1979 American League All-Star, Sid posted career highs in wins (twelve), appearances (seventy-six, second in the league), saves (nineteen) and strikeouts (108). On the way up, Sid also pitched in Honolulu during away games with Salt Lake City (a campaign that was good enough that it earned him his ticket to "The Show"). He started the '85 season in Nashville and finished in Honolulu and then retired. Since then, he's coached in the minors and, for years, in the Mexican Winter League, where he is currently the pitching coach for the Monterrey Sultans. In 2004, he was elected to Mexico's Baseball Hall of Fame.

Jerry Morales

Jerry Morales was a stellar starting outfielder during his only year as a Hawai'i Islander, 1971. He hit .272 and was in double digits for doubles, triples and homers. He'd done some similar damage against Hawai'i in 1970, swatting away for Don Zimmer's Salt Lake City Bees across the Pacific Coast League. Morales put in fifteen years at the major-league level (1969–83) with five teams and was a 1977 All-Star for the Cubbies, hitting .290 with power. Since retiring, he's coached in the minors and with the Expos/Nationals and scouted for the Dodgers.

Cotton Nash

Cotton Nash collected three hits during his big-league career (1967–70) with the White Sox and Twins. He did much better in the minors (nine years, 184 homers), where he played for the Islanders in 1964 and 1968 (outfield and first base). He also played plenty of road games at Honolulu while touring with Seattle, San Diego, Indy and Portland, for whom he hit thirty-seven dingers in '71.

But Cotton Nash is not included here for his baseball prowess; he is included because he is the only Hawai'i Islander who also played in the NBA. Nash was a forward with the Los Angeles Lakers and the San Francisco Warriors during the 1964–65 season, after which he jumped to the ABA to play for the Kentucky Colonels for one season more. He'd been an All-American hoopster at the fabled University of Kentucky.

Dick Nen

Dick Nen came up with the Dodgers in 1963, hit a homer in his first big-league game, manned first for the Senators from 1965 to 1967, played for the Cubs in 1968 and finished back in D.C. in 1970. He starred in Honolulu in 1965, swatting seventeen dingers in the first half of the season before the parent club came calling. He also hit plenty of homers at the Termite Palace for visiting Spokane from 1962 to 1964. Dick's son Robb was an All-Star closer for ten seasons in the majors.

Henry "Prince" Oana

Leafing through an old hardcover copy of the *Baseball Encyclopedia*, it'd be easy to overlook Hank Oana and his brief major-league career. But once you start drilling down to details, the story gets more and more curious until you finally have to abandon the reference book and uncover the rest of the story.

You'd see that in 1943 and 1945, Oana, a thirty-five-year-old rookie (which wasn't all that uncommon when most of the boys were in the service) pitched a mere thirteen games for the Detroit Tigers. But then, when you peer down to the batting section, you might notice that he also played outfield for the Phillies—nine years earlier, in 1934. And you'd see that this pitcher's lifetime average at the plate was .308, including three doubles, a triple, a homer and ten RBIs in just fifty-two at-bats!

And it's off to the races from there. Henry Kawaihoa Oana was born in Waipahu, making him the fourth Hawai'ian to hit "The Show" and the second in the National League. His mates nicknamed him "Prince," and although he didn't really have any royal blood, he made a royal mess of opponents in the minors. During his twenty-three-year career, which spanned four different decades, he rewrote all sorts of record books all over the mainland.

The baseball player formerly known as Prince broke in with the 1929 Globe Bears of the Arizona State League—still a teenager, he tore the cover off the horsehide. Oana hit .374 with twenty-six doubles, thirteen triples and eighteen homers in just 340 at-bats. He followed up by hitting .413 the following year with an even higher slugging percentage, earning a trip to the San Francisco Seals of the tougher Pacific Coast League, where he hit .326 with punch. He hit .345 the following year with the Seals and then .332 with Portland before getting his shot at the big leagues. For reasons unbeknownst to rational man, he got shipped back down and bounced around from Atlanta to Syracuse to Knoxville to Little Rock to Jackson (MS) to Fort Worth and up to Milwaukee before getting another shot at the bigs. Along the way, he hit over .300, including plenty homers, doubles and triples.

During this process, one of Oana's skippers—Hall of Famer Rogers Hornsby, no less—converted him to a pitcher. All he did was go 16-5 for the 1942 Forth Worth Cats (with a ludicrous 1.72 ERA) to get his ticket punched once again for major-league action.

Yet the management in Detroit didn't want to invest much time in a thirty-three-year-old semi-rookie, so they shipped him back down. But back he came in '45, only to find himself in Texas again for the '46 season. He responded by winning twenty-four ballgames on a sparkling 2.54 ERA (while also hitting .303 with power). The Prince hung around for five more seasons, pitching until the age of forty-one with Austin and, finally, Texarkana. He hit .375 and .348 as a player-manager there—probably selling tickets and popcorn, too.

Oana's minor-league totals? A .304 average with 2,292 base hits, 428 doubles, 130 triples, 261 homers, 1,368 RBIs to go along with eighty wins on the mound (in just eight full seasons of pitching) and a 3.24 ERA. He led his circuit in hits, homers, wins and other categories more than a dozen times.

Before all that, Oana was a five-sport star (baseball, football, basketball, track and swimming) at St. Louis High School in Honolulu, which was later attended by Benny Agbayani and UH coach Les Murakami, among others.

Barry Obama, shown here as a little lad sporting a University of Hawai'i shirt, took a good cut in hopes of trumping skeptical onlookers into believing that he actually *was* born on the Isles.

Barack Obama

Hawai'i native Barack Hussein Obama attended inner-city Punahou High, where he played on the basketball team. He acquired a love for baseball at an early age as well, attending a few Islanders games. Barry went on to become a U.S. senator in Illinois.

Joe Orsulak

Joe Orsulak played in the majors for fourteen seasons (1983–97) for five teams, hitting .300 for the 1985 Pirates. He earned his promotion for his 1983 numbers in Hawai'i: twelve doubles, thirteen triples, ten homers, thirty-eight steals, a .286 average and a good enough eye to strike out just forty-one times. During a part-year reprise in 1984, he posted similar numbers, and he returned for a few Vancouver away games in 1987. The Jersey native also played high school hoops and was an all-state soccer player.

Phil Ortega

Like Joe Moeller, Phil Ortega pitched for Hawai'i after being on Dodger pitching staffs with guys like Koufax and Drysdale. Phil was in the bigs for ten years: 1960–64 with Los Angeles, 1965–68 with Washington and a few games for the 1969 Angels. He was a key starter in D.C., winning in double digits (despite little support) three straight years. The big righty was a regular starter in Honolulu in 1969–70, playing away contests there for Spokane during the Islanders' first three seasons (1961–63). Ortega is a Native American—a Yaqui Indian, like fellow Hawai'i Islander Marty Perez.

Mitchell Page

If you look at Mitchell Page's 1977 rookie numbers (a .307 average to go along with twenty-one homers and forty-two steals), you'd wonder why the A's outfielder wasn't voted Rookie of the Year; that is, until you realize that Eddie Murray broke in that year, too. But Mitchell's numbers tumbled, and the A's released him six seasons later. He played a few games with the Pirates but got sent down to their farm team—the Hawai'i Islanders. Page's consistency on the Isles was mind-boggling: in both 1984 and 1985, he hit safely 39 times in 151 tries (a .258 clip) and had thirty-two RBIs. (He'd done better on road trips there with Tacoma in 1981–82, hitting .328 and .305, respectively.) He also pitched an inning for Hawai'i in '85, striking out one, giving up three earned runs (a 27.00 ERA!) and committing a balk. Mitchell then coached in the minors and with the Royals, Cards and Nationals. Ever versatile, he also had a small role in the Disney flick *Angels in the Outfield*.

Stan Palys

Stan Palys tore it up in Honolulu, smacking 50 homers over two seasons and batting better than .300 both times (.332 in '62 and .305 the following year). But the call didn't come (at thirty-three, he was deemed too old after four seasons with the Phils and Cincinnati), so he kept heading west and finished up with four seasons in Tokyo. His eleven seasons in the American minor leagues were noteworthy. To go along with a career average of .322, Palys racked up 189 home runs and 307 doubles, including several stellar seasons like 1960, when he owned the Southern Association—hitting .370 with 28 homers, 116 RBIs and 43 doubles).

Stan played a key role in one of the more unusual and controversial plays in Islanders' history. The hometown team was hosting the Spokane Indians at the Termite Palace, and visiting pitcher Bob Radovich happened to be tossing a no-hitter into the bottom of the ninth. Radovich walked Islander Ron Samford, and Palys went in to pinch run. Hawai'i first baseman Brown Taylor hit a grounder between first and second, and Palys let the ball hit him. According to the rulebook, he'd be called out (for interference) to end the game, but Taylor's grounder would be recorded as a base hit, spoiling the no-no. But as fate had it, league president Dewey Soriano happened to be in the stands that night, and he overruled the ruling on the field, stating that Stan's deed was intentionally unsportsmanlike. So it went down in the books as a fielder's choice, Taylor was the third out, and Radovich got credit for his no-hitter.

Joe Pepitone

Flamboyant Joe Pepitone made a brief stop in Hawai'i in 1976 to wrap up his career-ending comeback try; he hit one homer and batted .222 in thirteen games for the Islanders. Pepi had been an All-Star during his twelve seasons at "The Show," hitting 219 home runs and winning three Gold Gloves. From 1962 to 1969, Joe played for the Yankees until his antics exceeded his on-field contributions. He then bounced around from Houston to the Cubs and finally Atlanta (1973). He also played in Japan, where he occasionally showed up for games, and his name actually entered the lexicon as a sarcastic synonym for "slacker." But Joe was mostly famous in the late '60s for being baseball's version of Joe Namath—staying out too late to get anywhere near his potential.

Marty Perez

As noted in Phil Ortega's clip, Marty Perez is one of two Yaqui Indians who played for the Hawai'i Islanders; the two were teammates from 1969 to 1970. Marty was the starting shortstop, hitting a solid .280 in '69 and .281 in the championship run. His solid hitting and quick glove got him promoted, and he ultimately played ten seasons with five big-league clubs. Marty was a mainstay of the Braves' infield when Hank Aaron was breaking the Babe's career home run record.

Juan Pizarro

Juan Pizarro pitched in the majors for what seemed like forever. He played for eight teams over three decades—eighteen seasons in all. He was on back-to-back American League All-Star teams with the White Sox in 1963–64 and pitched in the 1957 and 1958 World Series for the Milwaukee Braves, winning a ring in '57. He didn't appear in the post-season again for sixteen years, but he did pull off a perfect closing appearance (at age thirty-seven) for the 1974 Pirates.

Amid all this, you might wonder how Juan found time to pitch for Hawai'i. But he did; this ancient mariner showed up just in time to lead the Islanders' 1970 championship push. Then thirty-three, Pizarro went a perfect 9-0, striking out sixty-seven in eighty-nine innings. (But he wasn't done with Honolulu yet; the following season, he came back to haunt his old teammates, winning nine for PCL rival

Tacoma.) The Puerto Rico native has been inducted into the Caribbean Confederation Hall of Fame and the Puerto Rican Sports Hall of Fame.

Tony Rego

Antone Rego, born in 1897 in Wailuku, became the second Hawai'i-born ballplayer to reach the Major Leagues. (Keep in mind that Hawai'i was a republic then, so he was actually coming from another country). And while Tony may have been number two from Hawai'i, he was the first Maui-born big-leaguer (later stars Kurt Suzuki and Shane Victorino also came from Wailuku). Rego was the son of Portuguese immigrants who had come over to work the sugar plantations and mills. The scrappy, diminutive catcher (five feet, four inches) joined the U.S. Navy and while stationed in Southern California signed a contract with the Pacific Coast League's Los Angeles Angels in 1920. He played for the St. Louis Browns from 1924 to 1925, swatting a Ted Williams–esque .406 over thirty-two at-bats in '25. In fourteen minor-league seasons (most with Los Angeles, the San Francisco Seals and the Portland Beavers in the PCL), Rego hustled his way to a .277 career mark and 102 doubles.

Jessie Reid

Jessie Reid, the seventh overall pick in the 1980 amateur draft, was born in Honolulu and played eight games for the Giants in 1987–88. Jessie played ten seasons in the Giants and A's organizations, swatting 111 home runs and swiping 157 bags, and then played four more years in Mexico and Japan. The strong, speedy outfielder's only big-league hit was a solo homer against the Padres that came in his fourth appearance.

Rick Renteria

Before Rick Renteria became the head coach of Mexico's national baseball team, he was the Padres bench coach and one of the final hitting stars for the Hawai'i Islanders. He'd played a few games there in 1984–85, but in '86, he hit .314 with twenty doubles and nine three-baggers. Rick also came back for the Islanders' final season the following year, playing away games for Calgary. In all, Renteria played twelve years in the minors, three in Mexico and five in the majors for Pittsburgh, Seattle and Florida. He's also managed plenty in the minors, where his son Anthony is currently playing.

Rick Reuschel

All-Star Rick Reuschel, who won 214 games over nine seasons, pitched for the Islanders in the middle of his major-league career. He did great during his 1985 rehab assignment in paradise, going 6-2 with a 2.50 ERA before being called back up to the National League. Rick broke in with the 1972 Cubs, where he was a mainstay for a decade (twenty wins in 1977) before playing for the Pirates and Giants (nineteen wins in 1988 at age thirty-nine). At age forty-two, he finally retired after winning a pair of Gold Gloves and placing third in Cy Young voting twice to complement his three trips to the All-Star Game. Rick also pitched in two World Series (1981, during his short-lived tenure with the Yanks, and again in 1988, for the earthquake-plagued Bay Bridge games against the A's) but didn't get a ring.

Rick's brother Paul, who pitched in tandem with his sib for the Cubs from 1975 to 1978, never pitched for the Islanders but pitched in Honolulu against them (Tacoma, 1971). As a Cub rookie, he relieved for Rick for a 7–0 shutout against the Dodgers—the only time in major-league history two brothers performed such a feat.

Tony Robello

Tony Robello got a couple cups of Kona coffee at "The Show"—an apt metaphor, actually, since he was the first guy born on the Big Island of Hawai'i (in the tiny sugar plantation town of Pahala) to make the Major Leagues. He was the third ballplayer from the island chain to make it to the majors and the first one to play in the National League. He played in the Cincinnati Reds' infield for sixteen games during 1933 and 1934, hitting .219. But Rego tore it up in the minors, leading his league in homers five times and accumulating a lifetime average of .327. Unfortunately, Tony was buried deep in the system for way too long; his ridiculously amazing 1939 season didn't get him a promotion. That year, Tony hit fifty-eight home runs at a .404 clip for the Pocatello Cards of the Pioneer League (which he was also managing at the tender age of twenty-six). He then scouted for the St. Louis Browns, Cardinals and Yankees before becoming a mainstay in the Cincinnati scouting troup for thirty seasons (until 1984). There, he stocked the world champion Big Red Machine with plenty of talent, including Hall of Famer Johnny Bench and fellow Hawai'ian Milt Wilcox.

Dave Roberts and Bob Davis made the 1975 Pacific Coast League All-Star team. Here, they await pre-game introductions at Hughes Stadium in Sacramento before the not-quite-sold-out crowd. (Roberts is in the middle, and Davis, wearing the tools of ignorance, is at the far right next to fellow catcher Art Kusnyer of the hometown Solons. Ironically, Dave played a lot more infield in Honolulu than catcher.)

Dave Roberts

Dave Roberts, not to be confused with pitcher Dave Roberts (whom he faced twenty-four times during his ten-year major-league career), hit twenty-one homers for the 1973 Padres. He also played for Texas, Houston and Philadelphia. David Wayne Roberts spent four seasons with the Islanders (1973–78), smacking thirty-one doubles in his all-star year, and wrapped up his career playing road games in Honolulu with Tucson in 1979. Meanwhile, David Arthur Roberts (who at least tried to undo some of the confusion by being a pitcher but compounded it by also playing for Houston and San Diego) was in the bigs from 1969 to 1981. And while he did not play for Hawai'i, he did close his career with the Phoenix Giants in '81, pitching some away games in Honolulu. He then coached for the Eugene Emeralds, where he'd played college ball as an Oregon Duck before being named to that state's sports hall of fame.

Floyd Robinson

In 1962, Floyd Robinson led the American League in doubles (forty-five) while hitting .312 and driving in 109 runs. The year before, he had hit .310, and two seasons later, he ended the year at .301. Floyd spent 1960–66 with the White Sox and then split the following two years with the Reds, A's and Red Sox. Robinson broke into the minors in 1954 at age eighteen and hit .318 with power and speed for the 1960 PCL San Diego Padres. He finished his career with the Islanders in 1969 as a starting outfielder who hit nineteen doubles and ten homers, stole thirteen bases and batted .266. Although Robinson's cousin Tommie Reynolds never played for Hawai'i, Tommie ironically spent more time there—putting in eight Coast League seasons' worth of away games with Islander opponents.

Buck Rodgers

Buck Rodgers managed fourteen seasons in the Major Leagues (1980–94) for teams that didn't like to spend a lot of money on talent (Milwaukee, Montreal and the Angels). However, to Buck's credit, he did finish above .500 (barely hanging on with 784 wins against 774 losses for a .503 clip). He also won the American League East in 1981, when his Brewers fell to the Yanks, and was named National League Manager of the Year in '87 for skippering his talent-free Expos to a third-place finish. Buck played nine seasons, all for the Angels, and caught Bo Belinsky's fabled no-hitter along the way. In 1969, Buck—by then veteran who knew how to handle pitchers—caught for the Islanders. After managing, he scouted for the Phillies for several seasons.

Lenn Sakata

Lenn Sakata, a Kalani High School Falcon, was the first Hawai'i native to play in a World Series (with the 1983 champion Baltimore Orioles). He played in the majors for eleven seasons after playing in Honolulu against the Islanders for Spokane, Vancouver and Tacoma. He broke into the majors with the 1977 Brewers and then manned a variety of infield positions for the A's and Yankees until 1987. Lenn skippered for several seasons in the minors and was named the California League Manager of the Year in 2005, when his San Jose Giants won the pennant. Sakata also managed his hometown Honolulu Sharks of the upstart Hawai'i Winter Baseball League. He's managed in Japan and recently returned to mainland U.S. soil to head the Modesto Nuts. Lenn is a member of the Hawai'i Sports Hall of Fame and is one of seven baseball players on the *Sports Illustrated*/CNN 1999 list of "The 50 Greatest Hawai'i Sports Figures," coming in at number thirty-two.

Chad Santos

Technically, Chad Santos has the highest lifetime major-league batting average of any Hawai'i-born ballplayer: he batted .429 (four for seven) with the 2006 Giants. This includes a homer, two RBIs and an .857 slugging percentage—not bad for three games' work. He smacked 115 dingers in the minors over nine seasons. Like Benny Agbayani, he attended St. Louis High in Honolulu and was initially drafted by the Royals.

Bronson Sardinha

Bronson Kiheimahanaomauiakeo Sardinha (say that three times fast) was the youngest of three brothers who signed pro contracts. All were born in Honolulu and attended Kamehameha High School (like Kanekoa Texeira). Bronson was drafted in the first round of the 2001 amateur draft (the thirty-fourth pick overall) and started strong, hitting .303 with power and speed for the Rookie League Gulf Coast Yanks. He climbed up the ranks, debuting on a roster that included names like future Hall of Famers Derek Jeter, Alex Rodriguez and Mariano Rivera against the arch-rival Red Sox at Boston's Fenway Park in late 2007. In just nine at-bats, he collected three hits (for a lifetime average of .333) and knocked in a pair of runs. But the Yankees outfield was loaded, of course, so he found himself in Akron in the spring of '08. Bronson hit .344 at Triple A Tacoma and .300 at Triple A Buffalo but found himself dropped to Double A Tulsa, where he hit .302 in 2011 and hung it up after that.

Dane Sardinha

Dane Kealoha Sardinha was the eldest of three brothers born in Honolulu and played prep ball for the Kamehameha Warriors. A catcher, he enjoyed the longest big-league career of the three—he debuted in 2006 and played for the Reds, Tigers and Phils for six seasons. In 2010, Dane smacked three homers in just thirty-nine at-bats for Philly. He shuttled between the bigs and minors most of those years; of his ten seasons in pro ball, Dane was at the Triple A level for seven. He'd been a college All-American at Pepperdine and was drafted by the Royals. While still in high school, he carried Team USA to a bronze medal at the 1996 World Junior Championship, leading the club in homers and RBIs.

Duke Sardinha

Like his brothers, Duke Sardinha was born in Honolulu and prepped at Kamehameha High. Duke also paved the way for Dane, playing college ball well enough at Pepperdine to earn a pro contract. He was drafted by the Rockies in 2001 but opted to stay in school. (Who could blame the guy? Pepperdine is in Malibu!) The Rockies tried again the following year, and Duke inked the deal. Unfortunately, the Rockies' brain trust couldn't figure out where to put him. Duke's seven-season minor-league career looks like an Abbott & Costello routine, as he played first, second and third base, outfield and even pitched a few ballgames. And ironically, during his only shot in Triple A (with the Colorado Springs club, which, even more ironically, had been the Hawai'i Islanders years before), Duke went a perfect one for one, batting 1.000.

Tom Satriano

Tom Satriano was an infielder for Hawai'i on the way up (1962–63) and a catcher on the way back down ('71). He was switched over to the latter role while in the big leagues. In between, he spent part of 1965 with Seattle, playing some away games in Honolulu. The USC grad belted twenty-one homers in his rookie campaign on the Isles and ended up playing ten seasons with the Angels and Red Sox as a backup backstop. He hit a homer in his first big-league at-bat, but the game was rained out, so it didn't count. His daughter Gina played for the professional Colorado Silver Bullets in the early '90s and was a teammate of Julie Croteau and Lee Anne Ketchum, who played in the Hawai'i Winter Baseball League.

Diego Segui

Diego Segui grew up playing baseball on another island—Cuba—and holds the honor of playing for the Islanders over the longest time span. Segui was on the original 1961 team, played again briefly in 1966 and wrapped up his career in Hawai'i in 1976—a sixteen-season spread. He also threw forkballs in the majors for fifteen years, leading the American League in ERA (2.56) for the 1970 A's and tossing a shutout inning to close a game in the 1975 World Series for the Red Sox.

Diego was still in need of some work on the way up in '61 (5-10), but Kansas City needed any available arm, so the Royals called him up early. The seasoning eventually worked. All those years later, along with Chuck Hartenstein, Diego was the Islanders' team ace in '76, going 11-5 at the age of thirty-eight. In 1978, he celebrated turning forty by embarking on an eight-year career in the Mexican League (after twenty-one seasons in U.S. pro ball) and tossing a perfect game. Segui finally retired after the 1985 season; he was forty-seven. His offseason exploits in the Venezuelan Winter League earned him a spot in that nation's hall of fame, and Diego is also a member of the Hispanic Heritage Museum Hall of Fame. His son David also went on to play in the majors, hitting better than .300 several times during his fifteen-year career.

Larry Sherry

Larry Sherry, at the tail end of his career, played just a few games for the Islanders in 1968, but in his second year with the Dodgers (1959), he was a star of the World Series. Larry was 2-0 with a ridiculous 0.71 ERA in that Fall Classic, finishing four games and earning two saves. He followed that with fourteen wins in 1960 and then played eight more seasons as a reliever for Los Angeles, Detroit, Houston and the Angels. His brother Norm caught for the Dodgers and Mets from 1959 to 1963, so for a while, they were the only brother battery in baseball. Larry also played a few away games in Hawai'i with Seattle (also in '68) and Tucson ('69) and later coached for the Pirates and Angels.

Tom Silverio

Tom Silverio was a mainstay in the Islanders' outfield during the successful 1969 and '70 campaigns, hitting .313 and .294, respectively. But after an offseason trade that saw him go to Salt Lake City, he came back to hit .339 against his former team, and he came back only to do more damage in '72. Silverio had brief appearances in the big leagues from 1970 to 1972 but didn't fare as well against the curve; Tom's lifetime average at "The Show" is an even .100. Silverio played pro ball for seventeen seasons, breaking in as a teen in 1965. He alternated between the minors and majors until 1972 and then headed south for a successful nine-year career in the Mexican League.

He finally retired in 1981. Tom's son Nelson played in the minors for several seasons and went on to coach for the Mets and manage the Dominican Republic national team. He currently manages an MLB player development program team in the Dominican Republic.

Jim Small

Bonus baby Jim Small broke in with Detroit in 1955 at the age of eighteen. He got his first hit off Hall of Famer (and future Hawai'i manager) Bob Lemon and batted .319 in limited action the following year. He stayed with the Tigers one more season and then played for the Kansas City A's in 1958. He was in the minors for the next few years, including a role as the number-five outfielder for the inaugural Islanders in 1961. He hit over .300 three times in the minors.

Tony Solaita

South Pacific hero Tony Solaita was born in Nuuuli, American Samoa, and first played organized ball in Hawai'i when his cousin invited him along to a Little League practice. He played seven years in the majors (1968–79) but had more success in Japan (155 homers in just four years, 1980–83) and the minors (167 home runs over eight seasons, 1965–73). He played a few games against the Islanders in 1969 while with Tucson—much to the delight of his large, loyal local following. (Hopes were high because he'd hit fifty-one homers the year before, forty-nine during the regular season and two more in the playoffs.) He also belted plenty of balls off another island during Puerto Rican Winter League ball. Tony's big-league career included stints with the Yankees, Royals, Angels, Expos and Jays. After retiring, Solaita returned to Samoa to take Little League teams to far-off places like Taiwan, the mainland United States and Hawai'i.

Jim Spencer

Jim Spencer played first base for fifteen major-league seasons (1968–82) with the Angels, Yankees, Rangers and A's. He was an All-Star in 1973 and won Gold Gloves in 1970 and '77. His best season (twenty-three homers and a .288 average) was with the 1979 Yanks after playing in his first World Series with the Bronx Bombers in '78. Spencer split 1969 between Hawai'i and the parent Angels, hitting .262 with six homers for the Islanders. His grandfather, Ben Spencer, played for the 1913 Washington Senators.

Don Stanhouse

At age thirty-two, Don Stanhouse ended his career as a closer for the Islanders in 1983. He had pitched in the majors for ten years (1972–82) with Texas, Montreal, Baltimore and the Dodgers. A 1979 All-Star for the Orioles, whom he helped reach the World Series, Don was known for unusual antics and drove managers nuts by pitching around so many batters. He'd pitched some away contests in Honolulu at the other end of his career, rehabbing with Spokane in 1973–74. His name is similar enough to the unrelated Dave Stenhouse, also an Islander alum, that it occasionally causes confusion.

Dave Stenhouse

Dave Stenhouse pitched three seasons for the Senators, winning eleven ballgames as a rookie in 1962. In fact, he started the second All-Star Game that year. He finished his career with three years (1965–67) in Honolulu, where he won four games for the Islanders, mostly pitching in relief. During his minor-league career, Stenhouse won twelve or more games in six different years, including 1958, when he went 16-8 with a 2.91 ERA. After retiring, he served as the head coach at Brown University from 1981 to 1990. Dave's son Mike also played at "The Show," spending five seasons with the Expos, Twins and Red Sox before becoming an Expos radio announcer. Dave's other son, Dave Jr., played five seasons in the Toronto organization.

Bob Strampe

Bob Strampe pitched for the Islanders during two seasons in the mid-70s. In 1975, he won twelve, whiffed 120 and led the Hawai'i staff with thirteen complete games. Bob got into seven games for the 1972 Tigers. His eight-year minor-league career (1969–76) also included away-game stops in Honolulu. His dad pitched in the minors in 1934.

Kurt Suzuki

Maui native Kurt Suzuki, the starting A's catcher for several seasons, started out with the Baldwin High Bears in Wailuku. Kurt broke in with Oakland in 2007 and played five seasons there before going to the Nationals. His best season so far is 2009, when he had thirty-seven doubles, fifteen homers, eighty-eight RBIs and a .274 batting average. He knocked in a couple runs for the Nats in their 2012 post-season series against the Cards. In mid-2013, Washington dealt him back to Oakland. Suzuki is known as one of the top-fielding backstops in the game. He played in the 2004 College World Series for perennial powerhouse Cal State Fullerton, knocking in the Titans' game-winning run in the championship.

Derek Tatsuno

Pitcher Derek Tatsuno set NCAA records for wins (twenty, still standing) and strikeouts (234, still standing) at the University of Hawai'i in 1979. (Before that, he was 27-1 with a 0.34 ERA at Aiea High.) Tatsuno went on to play in Japan but developed arm trouble, and by the time he came back to sign a major-league contract, it was too late. He spent a few years in the minors, finally finishing up with the Islanders during their last two seasons. Tatsuno was so dominant at Manoa that he was elected to the College Baseball Hall of Fame, and his jersey number (sixteen) was retired by the university. Derek is also one of seven baseball players on the *Sports Illustrated*/CNN 1999 list of "The 50 Greatest Hawai'i

Sports Figures," placing ninth overall. He's the highest-placed honoree who made it primarily on his baseball prowess (Herm Wedemeyer came in higher but was mostly included for his football skills), which is even more impressive considering he never got to pitch in the Major Leagues.

Kanekoa Texeira

Maui-born Kanekoa Texeira joined cousin Shane Victorino in the majors in 2010. After Kanekoa came up with Seattle, the Royals picked him up, and he collected his first big-league win for Kansas City. Kanekoa wore number fifty for the Royals (as have a few of his other Hawai'i-native mates) to honor the Islands' statehood. He starred at Kamehameha High (like fellow Warrior alums the Sardinha brothers) and was drafted by the Brewers, but he declined. The White Sox then drafted him in 2006 out of junior college in California. He pitched extremely well in the ChiSox organization, working his way up the ladder for three seasons with ERAs of 0.76, 0.93 and 2.01 before being traded to the Yankees. After two years in the Yanks' system, he was drafted by the Mariners. He's subsequently pitched in the Reds organization, and he started 2013 in the independent Atlantic League before being picked up by Triple A Louisville in the International League.

Bobby Thigpen

In 1990, armed with a 1.83 ERA, Bobby Thigpen set a major-league single-season record for saves (fifty-seven) that lasted eighteen years. However, he started all the games he pitched with the final-season 1987 Hawai'i Islanders. During his All-Star career in the majors, Bobby was one of the game's dominant closers. He also pitched some shutout ball in the 1993 World Series for the Phillies. He played eight years for the White Sox, starting in 1986, and retired after the 1994 season with the Mariners. After that, he played in Japan and staged a 1996 comeback with Nashville in the American Association before ongoing injuries ended his career prematurely. Thigpen then coached and managed in the minors, and he's currently the bullpen coach for his old ChiSox.

Mark Thurmond

Mark Thurmond won twelve games as an ace of the Islanders' 1982 staff, earning a ride to San Diego. He pitched for the Padres from 1983 to 1986 and then played four seasons more with Detroit, Baltimore and the Giants. His best year was 1984, when he went 14-8 with a nice 2.97 ERA for the Padres and got to pitch in the World Series.

Jerry Turner

Jerry Turner was a one-man wrecking crew for the 1975 Islanders, earning himself a trip up to San Diego. He hit .329 with plenty of punch, stole bases and knocked in runs. Jerry started in the Padre outfield for the rest of the '70s and then had stints with the White Sox and Detroit before returning to San Diego to wrap up his big-league career in 1983. He hung on to split a season between Portland and Las Vegas in the PCL, playing some final away games in Honolulu Stadium against his old Islanders.

Bobby Valentine

Most fans think of Bobby Valentine as a manager (Rangers, 1985–92; Mets, 1996–2002; and the ill-fated Red Sox experiment of 2012), but he was also a star for the Islanders in 1976, hitting .304 with a little power. He'd played in Honolulu against the Islanders with Spokane (1969–71) and Salt Lake (1975). In the majors, Bobby played shortstop, second, third and outfield for the Dodgers and four other teams from 1969 to 1979. (He also caught two games, the record will note.) Mr. Valentine took his 2000 Mets to the World Series and kept his Pacific ties going by managing the Chiba Lotte Marines in Japan in 1995 and from 2004 to 2009 (winning the championship in '05).

Fred Valentine

Fred Valentine was the Islanders' star in 1965, hitting .324 with twenty-five homers. It was his only year with the club, as he was in the midst of a seven-season big-league career. His numbers earned him a trip back to "The Show," and he responded by picking up some MVP votes after a stellar 1966 with the Senators. "Squeaky" stole twenty-two bags, ranking tops in the American League with an 85 percent success rate on the base paths. Before (and after) that, he played for the Orioles, starting in 1959 and finishing in 1968. He'd been a two-sport star at Tennessee State, where he also played quarterback and received several NFL offers. He finished playing baseball in Hanshin (1970) and later became a vice-president of the MLB Players Alumni Association.

Shane Victorino

All-Star Shane Victorino is today's most prominent Hawai'i-born baseball player. His clutch post-season heroics for the 2013 Red Sox are now part of the game's history. His seventh-inning grand slam in Game 6 of the ALCS propelled Boston past Detroit and into the World Series, and his bases-loaded double at Fenway knocked in the World Series–winning run against the Cards. Yet that wasn't the Golden Glove winner's first trip to the Fall Classic—he also won a ring with the Phillies in 2008 (the same season he won the Lou Gehrig Award). Shane hit his ninetieth big-league homer at the end of 2012—significant because it tied Mike Lum for most major-league home runs smacked by a Hawai'i native. But Shane broke the tie early in 2013, and now every time he chalks up a dinger, he breaks his own record (which is now over one hundred). Shane has also played for the Padres and Dodgers. His community work with children resulted in his winning the Branch Rickey Award in 2011, and he's also bolstered his Hawai'i ties with a guest appearance on *Hawai'i Five-0*. The Flyin' Hawai'ian went to St. Anthony High in Wailuku, Maui, winning three state track titles (and setting a state record in the one-hundred-meter dash) for the Trojans.

Brandon Villafuerte

Born in Hilo on the Big Island, Brandon Villafuerte pitched for five major-league teams over four seasons. He was drafted by Florida out of high school but didn't sign. But the following year, he inked with the Mets. Brandon broke in for the Tigers in 2000, played the next season with Texas and finally enjoyed a full rookie season with the Padres the following year. Brandon was a solid closer in 2002, finishing eleven games and posting a remarkable 1.41 ERA. He repeated with the Pads in 2003 and then went to Arizona for '04. While with Texas, he wore number fifty in honor of his birth state. In all,

Villafuerte logged sixteen seasons in the pros, starting at age nineteen and wrapping up at age thirty-five in 2011. As a closer, he also boasts an amusing career minor-league batting stat: in 643 games, he had only twenty-nine at-bats! He struck out nearly one thousand batters during his career.

Leon Wagner

"Daddy Wags" was an All-Star in 1962 and 1963, highlighting a twelve-year career (1958–69) with five teams. He hit 37 homers for the '62 Los Angeles Angels, 31 for Cleveland in '64 and 211 in all. He finished his career in the PCL, playing away games for Phoenix in Honolulu (1969–70) before joining the Islanders in 1971. He hit nine homers in a half season that year, bringing his minor-league total to 154 (and his pro total to 365). His eight-year minor-league average is .308. After retiring, Leon appeared in a couple movies, and he liked Hawai'i so much that he stayed there to sell cars for a few years.

Bozo Wakabayashi

Hawai'i native Bozo Wakabayashi was the first Nisei to play in Japan's major leagues. (His mama called him Tadashi—it was the guys who brandished him the less-flattering moniker.) He was born in 1908 and starred for Honolulu's McKinley High School Tigers in the late '20s. Bozo visited Japan to play exhibition ball and was so good that he was recruited by a school to stay, which he did. Over the course of seventeen years in the Japanese Baseball League, from 1936 to 1953 (when he was forty-five), he received two MVP awards (1944 and 1947). Over the last eight years, he was a player-manager and won a pennant. After that, he coached for several seasons more. Over his pitching career, Bozo won 243 games, struck out an even one thousand and finished with a remarkable 1.99 ERA. He helped himself at the plate, too, collecting more than two thousand hits. He was the first Hawai'ian player named to the Japanese Baseball Hall of Fame, and he also belongs to the Hawai'ian Sports Hall of Fame.

Bob Walk

Bob Walk had the third-worst name for a pitcher in major-league history (behind Boom-Boom Beck and Homer Bailey), but the 1988 All-Star had a pretty good career. He won 105 ballgames over fourteen seasons (1980–93) with the Phils, Braves and Pirates. Bob won a World Series ring as a rookie (with Philly) but never made it back to the Fall Classic. He spent a couple rehab years in Hawai'i, going 9-5 with a 2.26 ERA in 1984 and 16-5 with a 2.65 clip in '85. He's been broadcasting Pirates games for twenty years now.

U.L. Washington

U.L. Washington's career is mostly uneventful, although he is interesting for a few reasons. First, there's the name. U.L. stands for...U.L. Then there's the toothpick; yep, he's the guy who always played with a sliver of wood dangling from his face. And he wore number zero for the Pirates in 1986. U (as we will call him for short) played for the Islanders in 1986, batting all of .242. He played in the majors for eleven years (1977–87) with the Royals, Pirates and Expos, playing in the 1980 World Series for Kansas City. Mr. Washington subsequently coached and managed in the minors, and he's currently with the Red Sox organization.

Eddie Watt

Eddie Watt got World Series rings with the Orioles in 1966 and 1970, also appearing in 1969 and 1971. A reliever, he pitched for Baltimore, Philly and the Cubs from 1966 to 1975. After that, Eddie was a mainstay in the Hawai'i bullpen in 1976–77. He famously snapped the team out of a slump in late '77, throwing the resin bag (rather than the ball) to the plate. Eddie later coached and managed in the minors.

Justin Wayne

Justin Wayne pitched for Florida from 2002 to 2004. He and his older brother, Hawkeye, were both born in Honolulu and attended local schools. (Hawkeye was his real name, by the way, not a nickname. He pitched in the minors from 1999 to 2002.) Their dad, Jeff, played college ball for SUNY before becoming a prominent attorney on the Isles. Justin signed with Montreal while attending Stanford and also played in the Dodgers organization. While at Stanford, he helped lead the Cardinal to the College World Series. He was named co-Pac-10 Pitcher of the Year in 2000, and he's at the top of the list for several of the university's career pitching categories.

Herm Wedemeyer

Hilo-born Herm Wedemeyer was a baseball star at St. Louis High in Honolulu and went to college in California on an athletic scholarship. Herm earned a tryout with the San Francisco Seals of the old Pacific Coast League and in 1950 played outfield for the Salt Lake City Bees, hitting a respectable .250 as a rookie in the Pioneer League. But that was just his hobby. Herm also played football, and he was named a college All-American (finishing fourth in 1945 Heisman Trophy voting). He played professionally for the Los Angeles Dons and Baltimore Colts and later was elected to the College Football Hall of Fame and the Hawai'i Sports Hall of Fame. (His younger brother, Charlie, was also a football star, playing at Michigan State. Another brother, John, played minor-league baseball in 1941.)

But Wedemeyer still had other careers in mind. He spent several years on the Honolulu City Council and in the Hawai'i House of Representatives, and he was also a regular on the original *Hawai'i Five-0*, playing Detective Duke Lukela from 1971 to 1980. Later on, he guest-starred on another Hawai'i-based TV show, *Magnum, P.I.* For his combined athletic exploits, Herm was named to the *Sports Illustrated*/CNN 1999 list of "The 50 Greatest Hawai'i Sports Figures." Ranked at number six overall, he's the highest-ranked baseball guy on the list.

Johnny Werhas

Third-sacker Johnny Werhas was a fan favorite in Honolulu for several seasons. In 1969, he hit .298, knocked out 15 homers and drove in 90 runs. In the championship season that followed, he put up similar numbers—and he did it again in '72 (19 homers this time) before coming back for a final half season in 1973 and retiring at age thirty-five. Yet fans at the Termite Palace already knew Johnny well; he'd been beating their Islanders for five seasons (with Spokane and San Diego), chalking up batting averages like .306 and .309 to go along with plenty of home runs. In thirteen minor-league seasons, he finished with 151 homers and 1,445 hits.

Werhas actually went back to Hawai'i in an unusual way; he'd played in Japan in 1971, and his Taiyo Whales swapped him to the Islanders for Clete Boyer—the first time such an international deal had been struck.

Johnny played three seasons (1964–67) with the Dodgers and Angels, after being an All-American across town at USC. He turned in his flannels to be a man of the cloth and is now pastoring a church in Southern California.

Milt Wilcox

Milt Wilcox, born in Honolulu, pitched in the majors for sixteen seasons, breaking in with the 1970 Reds. He played in the World Series that fall with the Big Red Machine and again for the 1984 Tigers (a winning effort). In '84, Milt went 17-8 en route to winning 119 games overall. He also pitched for the Indians, Cubs and Mariners through 1986, winning eleven or more games seven straight seasons at "The Show." Wilcox pitched in the minors for eight seasons, starting in 1968 at the age of eighteen. And despite playing six of those seasons at the Triple A level, he never worked in the PCL to make it back to his Hawai'ian hometown.

Jerome Williams

Jerome Williams began his career as a starter but is now a middle reliever for the Angels. He was born in Honolulu and went to Waipahu High (Waipahu borders Pearl Harbor), where he was so good for the Marauders that the Giants made him a first-round pick (thirty-ninth overall) in the 1999 amateur draft. Jerome debuted for the big club in 2003 as a member of the starting rotation, posting a solid ERA of 3.30. He won ten ballgames in his sophomore season, went to the Cubs for two years and then put in a year for the Nationals before heading west to Orange County. There, the team has gradually transitioned him more and more toward the bullpen, and it's paid off. He's now a key member of the Angel's pitching staff.

Jerome is occasionally confused with the NBA alum of the same name, but they're definitely different people—the six-inch height difference is a good tip-off, if you will pardon the expression. A true Islandballer at heart, our Jerome Williams has played winter ball in Puerto Rico and on Taiwan. He wears a puka shell necklace while pitching and is the ultimate representation of Hawai'i's trans-Pacific, multi-cultural ethnic mixing pot, claiming Hawai'ian, Chinese, Portuguese, Spanish, Japanese, Norwegian, African, Filipino and American heritage.

Johnnie Williams

Honolulu Johnnie was his nickname—quite appropriate for the first Hawai'i-born Major League Baseball player, way back in 1914. Johnnie Williams was born in the Kingdom of Hawai'i in 1889. He played for St. Louis High School (later attended by Benny Agbayani, Chad Santos and Brandon

League) and came up with the 1911 Sacramento Solons (then known as the Sacts). He pitched there four years, moving with the team as they became the San Francisco Missions, before being drafted by the Detroit Tigers. He appeared in half a dozen games alongside Ty Cobb.

Williams went back to the Pacific Coast League and played briefly for the Los Angeles Angels (then merely known as the Los Angeles Angels—nothing about Anaheim, Orange County, California or Disneyland) and Salt Lake City Bees before joining the Hawai'i Infantry and entering World War I. Once he came home to Hawai'i, Williams barnstormed around the Pacific Rim, playing semipro ball and leading groups to Japan. To cap off his career, the Hawai'i Islanders (which had just moved out from Sacramento) invited him to be honored at their inaugural home game at Honolulu Stadium in 1961.

Walt Williams

Some might remember Walt Williams's nickname: No-Neck. (It becomes self-explanatory when you look at an old Topps card of the five-foot-six fireplug.) Nonetheless, the scrappy outfielder broke in with the Houston Colt .45s in 1964 and played ten seasons at "The Show," also suiting up with the White Sox, Indians and Yankees. He hit .304 for the ChiSox in 1969 and throughout his career helped his teams by hardly ever striking out (due in part to his smaller-than-normal strike zone). He whiffed just 33 times in '69, compared to Reggie Jackson's 142. A year earlier, he had torn the cover off the ball for Hawai'i, batting .319 with punch and speed. In 1966, he'd done the same against the Islanders, hitting .330 (with fifty-four doubles!) for a Pacific Coast League team from Tulsa. From 1976 to 1979, he played in Japan and Mexico, later managing in the minors and coaching for his old White Sox.

Ron Wotus

Ron Wotus rotated between Hawai'i and the Pittsburgh Pirates in 1983 and

1984 and then spent all of 1986 with the Islanders. In '83, he hit .301 with power, earning a late-season call-up, and in '86 he hit .315. Ron managed in the minors for seven seasons, finishing first three times. He was named Pacific Coast League Manager of the Year in 1997 (with the Phoenix Firebirds) and received a promotion to be the San Francisco Giants' bench coach. He's held that spot for more than a decade, thus owning a pair of World Series rings (2010 and 2012).

Tyler Yates

Tyler Kali Yates is one of the few Kaua'i-native big-leaguers. Born in Lihu'e, he attended Kaua'i High School (go Chicken Hawks!) before pitching at the University of Hawai'i's Hilo campus on the Big Island. Ty was drafted by the A's in 1998, broke in with the Mets in 2004 and played for the Braves and Pirates from 2006 to 2009. He appeared in seventy-five games in '07 (when he whiffed sixty-nine batters in sixty-six innings) and seventy-two contests in '08. Obviously a hard-throwing closer, the six-foot-four righty has returned to his roots and is now coaching his old high school baseball team (popularly known as the Red Raiders rather than their official moniker). His younger brother Kirby was drafted by the Red Sox in 2005 and has worked his way up to Triple A, where he's pitching well (career ERA around 2.70, with way more than one strikeout per inning pitched).

Bill Yohe

Bill Yohe wasn't born in Hawai'i (he came over from Illinois as a lad), but he graduated from Farrington High School in Honolulu and made it to the Major Leagues in 1909. So although not technically a native, he could be considered the first local product to hit the big time. (John Matias also attended Farrington, a mere six decades later, with Wally Yonamine in between.) Yohe, a five-foot-eight third baseman, got into twenty-one games for the 1911 Washington Senators. He'd barnstormed around and played on semipro teams before finally signing a minor-league contract and suiting up professionally at the age of twenty-seven, in 1906. He was a slick-fielding team leader—evidenced by the fact that he'd already served as a player-manager before being called up. Like a lot of journeymen in the day, Bill played pretty much everywhere—highlighted by a stop for the Moose Jaw Robin Hoods of the Western Canada League. He finally retired after the 1915 season at age thirty-six.

Wally Yonamine

Wally Yonamine: biography-worthy ballplayer.

Maui-born Wally Yonamine was a teammate of Herm Wedemeyer on the 1950 Salt Lake City Pioneers, hitting .335 with power that season. He was born in the tiny village of Olowalu and attended both Farrington High School (in Honolulu) and Lahainaluna High (in Lahaina, back on Maui). Like Herm, Wally was a true two-sport star. He played pro football for the San Francisco 49ers, becoming the first Japanese American in the NFL—not bad for a guy who stood five feet, nine inches tall. He achieved his greatest baseball success playing in Japan (at the urging of San Francisco Seals manager Lefty O'Doul), where he was an eleven-time all-star who hit .311 while playing from 1951 to 1962 with the Yomiuri Giants and Chunichi Dragons. Wally led his teams to four championships, and he was the 1957 Japan Central League MVP. He was also the first foreigner to manage in the Japanese major leagues, heading Chunichi from 1972 to 1977. Yet his success went beyond the numbers. As a Nisei, Wally was the first American-born player in Japan after the war, and he encountered some of the same attitudes that Jackie Robinson faced in the States. His hustling style and stellar performance won over even his harshest critics, as he ultimately was the first foreign-born player elected to the Japanese Baseball Hall of Fame. Back in Honolulu, he's also been enshrined in the Hawai'i Sports Hall of Fame, and he's one of seven baseball players on the *Sports Illustrated*/CNN 1999 list of "The 50 Greatest Hawai'i Sports Figures," coming in at number twenty-two.

Bibliography

Bainbridge, Jim. *The 70-Year Road Trip*. Bloomington, IN: Solution Tree, 2007.

Cisco, Dan. *Hawai'i Sports: History, Facts, and Statistics*. Honolulu: University of Hawai'i Press, 1999.

Okihiro, Michael. *AJA Baseball in Hawai'i: Ethnic Pride and Tradition*. Honolulu: Hawai'i Hochi, 1999.

Subica, Wayne. *Historic Hoolulu Park—Hilo, Hawai'i*. Kearney, NE: Morris Publishing, 2008.

Suehiro, Arthur. *Honolulu Stadium: Where Hawai'i Played*. Honolulu: Watermark Publishing, 2008.

Tominaga, Lance. *Catch the Dream: The Story of Hawai'i Winter Baseball*. Honolulu: Watermark Publishing, 2006.

INDEX

I

J

K

N

O

P

Y

Z

About the Author

Jim Vitti writes books about baseball and islands (like *Chicago Cubs: Baseball on Catalina Island* and *Brooklyn Dodgers in Cuba*), and he won the 2004 Sporting News/Society for American Baseball Research Award. As a kid, watching the Islanders play in Sacramento, he wished he could see their home games, too.

Visit us at
www.historypress.net

This title is also available as an e-book